McLAR

C000173015

Other books by this author:

WILLIAMS
Formula 1 Racing Team

BENETTON
Formula 1 Racing Team

McLAREN
The epic years

FIFTY YEARS OF FERRARI
A grand prix and
sports car racing history

FERRARI
The battle for revival

DAMON HILL
On top of the world

WILLIAMS
Triumph out of tragedy

WILLIAMS
The business of grand prix racing

DAMON HILL
From zero to hero

THE QUEST FOR SPEED
Modern racing car design
and technology

DRIVING FORCES
Fifty men who have shaped
motor racing

McLAREN

FORMULA 1 RACING TEAM

Alan Henry

Haynes Publishing

© Alan Henry 1999

All rights reserved. No part of this book may be reproduced or
transmitted in any form or by any means, electronic or mechanical,
including photocopying, recording or by any information storage or
retrieval system, without written permission from the publisher.

First published in November 1999

A catalogue record for this book is
available from the British Library

ISBN: 1 85960 425 0

Library of Congress catalog card no. 99-73262

Haynes North America Inc.,
861 Lawrence Drive, Newbury Park,
California 91320, USA.

Published by Haynes Publishing, Sparkford,
Nr Yeovil, Somerset BA22 7JJ, UK.

Tel: 01963 440635 Fax: 01963 440001
Int. tel: +44 1963 440635 Fax +44 1963 440001
E-mail: sales@haynes-manuals.co.uk
Web site: www.haynes.co.uk

Designed and typeset by G&M, Raunds, Northamptonshire
Printed and bound in Great Britain by J. H. Haynes and Co. Ltd, Sparkford

Contents

Acknowledgements

This is a totally new book even though some of its factual content owes much to my previous volume *McLaren: The epic years* (Haynes, 1998). However, I would like to thank Ron Dennis, Adrian Newey, Martin Whitmarsh, Anna Guerrier, Nancy Edwards and everybody at McLaren International for allowing me to get close enough to their racing team at various Grands Prix over the years to get what I hope is an accurate perspective on their operations. I would also like to thank Norbert Haug, the Mercedes-Benz motorsport director, and Wolfgang Schattling for their unstinting help and assistance. John Townsend of Formula 1 Pictures and David Phipps also have my appreciation for their prompt and efficient efforts when it came to illustrating this volume.

Alan Henry
Tillingham, Essex
November 1999

Introduction

Saving the best until last, Mika Hakkinen scored a faultless victory in the 1999 Japanese Grand Prix to become only the seventh driver in the 50-year history of the World Championship to win the crown two years running. Starting from second place on the grid, he accelerated into an immediate lead ahead of Michael Schumacher's Ferrari and kept the upper hand throughout the 53-lap race to win by just over five seconds.

It was a moment of pure relief for Hakkinen and the team after a season dogged by problems, many of their own making. A combination of team orders, mechanical failures and driver errors had lost him more than 50 points. In the build-up to Suzuka, while the Finn looked strained, Ferrari – reinstated after their Malaysian disqualification – and in particular his rival Eddie Irvine, appeared swaggeringly confident. But the best man won.

Hakkinen went into the race four points behind Irvine and emerged two points ahead, the Ulsterman finishing an outdriven third. Yet McLaren lost its Constructors' Championship to Ferrari, partly due to David Coulthard having an unfortunate spin in the other MP4/14 challenger and then retiring with gearbox trouble.

McLaren started the 1999 season with high hopes for the new MP4/14, powered by the latest, upgraded Mercedes F0110H V10 engine.

The season opened in Melbourne where Hakkinen and Coulthard seemingly found themselves operating on another planet from the opposition. Having buttoned up the front row of the grid they grabbed an early lead, pulling clear at over a second a lap. But this time it didn't last.

Hakkinen, who'd been obliged to take the spare car at the start after his own developed a misfire, just squeezed ahead of Coulthard going into the first corner. But the Scot quickly detected that Mika looked a little uncertain with his new mount, so he decided to sit back and wait for his opportunity. Unfortunately, gearchange gremlins intervened and David came coasting into the pits for good after only 14 laps.

'My car was running perfectly when all of a sudden I couldn't downchange at the fast chicane and got stuck in sixth gear,' he shrugged. Then it was Hakkinen's turn to hit trouble.

On lap 15 the safety car was deployed after Jacques Villeneuve's British American 01 lost its rear wing and spun into a barrier. At a stroke Hakkinen's 18sec lead was wiped out as Irvine moved into the queue behind him, with Heinz-Harald Frentzen's Jordan and Ralf Schumacher's Williams following after.

Once the Villeneuve debris was cleared the pack got the green light to start racing again at the end of lap 17, but very soon Hakkinen knew he was in trouble. On the sprint down to the first corner the Finn was engulfed by his rivals as the McLaren's throttle actuation went haywire. Next time round he was in the pits.

'We plugged in a computer to see what the problem was,' said technical director Adrian Newey. 'We tried to disengage some functions in an effort to cure the problem and sent him back into the race. But it didn't work.' Mika lasted another five laps before calling it a day and eventual winner Eddie Irvine's Ferrari surged into the lead.

It seemed as though 'Irv's' appearance at the head of the Championship table was nothing more than a temporary setback for the McLaren squad. Hakkinen duly put the team back on the top step of the victory podium when he scored the tenth victory of his Formula 1 career in round two, the Brazilian Grand Prix, after a fine and controlled tactical team effort.

Mika beat Michael Schumacher's Ferrari into second place by 4.9 sec while Frentzen was third ahead of Ralf Schumacher and Irvine who now led the championship with 12 points after two races, ahead of Hakkinen and Frentzen on ten apiece.

The Finn comfortably had the legs on all his key rivals with the exception of his luckless team-mate David Coulthard who, having joined him on the front row, failed to finish after a duff gearbox rounded off a day which saw his engine stall on the grid and caused his brief, belated appearance in the race three laps behind the rest of the field.

It seemed as though the McLaren team was back on track, but Mika made an inexplicable mistake while leading in the opening stages of the San Marino Grand Prix, crashing out of the race and leaving Coulthard with the task of grappling Michael Schumacher's Ferrari round Imola.

It was a difficult race for David and he got some bad breaks in among the slower traffic. But it was all too easy to blame the backmarkers. Although they did him no favours, David was not sufficiently decisive. His team was beaten on strategy and Michael Schumacher out-drove the popular Scot.

The result was a memorable victory by four seconds for the Ferrari team leader, the 34th of his career, which now put him into the lead of the drivers' World Championship after only three races. He played it cool in the opening stages, then made his first refuelling stop on lap 31 while Coulthard stayed out for another four laps.

Taking into account the two drivers' refuelling stops, Schumacher made up a crucial seven seconds on Coulthard during this period of the race. It saw him get ahead of the McLaren driver when Coulthard made his sole refuelling stop, after which the Ferrari team leader was able to open up a 21.8sec lead which saw him through his second 'splash and dash' refuelling stop without losing his advantage.

Yet Coulthard was not convinced. 'I think my one stop strategy would have been good enough (to win) if I had not had problems in traffic,' he said thoughtfully. 'It seemed as though people were particularly uncooperative with me. I appreciate other drivers have their own races to run but I think they should have been prepared to lose a second or so to let the leaders past.'

Now the points table looked very different with Schumacher on 16, Irvine on 12 and Hakkinen on 10.

Mika qualified on pole at Monaco, but Schumacher's Ferrari got the jump on him from the start and ran away to win unchallenged for the second time in a fortnight, with Irvine in second place. It was the first time Ferrari had posted a one-two victory through the streets of the principality in the 57-year history of the race.

Hakkinen was almost half a minute behind Schumacher when he took to the escape road at the tricky downhill Mirabeau corner, just beyond Casino Square, after skidding on oil dropped by Toranosuke Takagi's Arrows which had suffered a major engine failure. 'The incident must have just happened when I arrived,' said Mika. 'When I tried to turn into Mirabeau the rear wheels began to lock, so I decided to steer down the escape road rather than risk spinning into the barrier.

'I made a really bad start, with too much wheelspin and during the race I suffered with inconsistent handling coupled with a very heavy steering load which probably means I had some sort of front end failure.'

Mika Hakkinen, only the seventh driver in F1 history to win consecutive World Championships, shares the triumph with the McLaren team whose calm strategy and faultless pitstops helped him take victory in Japan. (Formula One Pictures)

A detailed and probing post-race examination revealed that there was nothing obviously wrong with the car. Schumacher now had 26 points, Irvine 18, Hakkinen 14 and Coulthard six.

It was therefore not before time when Hakkinen and Coulthard firmly put a stop to Ferrari's winning streak by storming to a one-two finish in the Spanish Grand Prix, dominating the rostrum for the first time since the previous year's German Grand Prix.

Hakkinen, who qualified brilliantly on pole in the final moments of Saturday's qualifying session, stamped his mastery on the race from the word go. The Finn led all but four of the 65 laps, only relinquishing the advantage fleetingly to Coulthard when he made his two routine refuelling stops.

During the middle sector of the race Coulthard was frustrated by a handling inconsistency which lost him a lot of time, allowing Schumacher's Ferrari to close within a second at one point. He also did little to help his own cause by momentarily over-shooting his pit at the first refuelling stop, which cost an extra five seconds he could ill afford.

Schumacher 30 points, Hakkinen 24, Coulthard 12. It was beginning to look slightly more comfortable.

Michael had won two on the trot and now it was Mika's turn to back up the Spanish success with a fine victory in the Canadian Grand Prix. He picked his way through the barrage of spins, crashes, collisions and penalties which bedevilled most of his rivals to score a convincing victory at the Circuit Gilles Villeneuve which put him into the lead of the 1999 title contest for the first time.

Heinz-Harald Frentzen seemed on course to take a fine second place in this race of changing fortunes, but his Jordan Mugen-Honda crashed heavily on lap 66. This was caused by a brake disc exploding, and the capacity crowd was treated to the remarkable spectacle of a World Championship grand prix finishing with the safety car leading the field round the final lap at much-reduced speed. That left Giancarlo Fisichella's Benetton to finish second ahead of Irvine, Ralf Schumacher and Johnny Herbert's Stewart-Ford. Frentzen eventually staggered away from his damaged car after being badly stunned by the 150mph impact.

The number of incidents was certain to re-ignite the controversy over the lack of grip developed by the current grooved tyres and the manner in which they aggravated the aerodynamic instability of these narrow-track cars when running in close company.

After qualifying second on the grid Hakkinen ran second from the start until he was presented with an unexpected bonus when Michael Schumacher, who had led from pole position, made a rare error and smashed into a concrete retaining wall.

Hakkinen now led the championship with 34 points to Schumacher's 30; Coulthard 12. The race had brought no better luck for the beleaguered Scot who finished seventh after colliding with Irvine, and being docked a 10sec stop-go penalty for mistakenly overtaking the safety car out on the circuit.

Back to Europe again for the French Grand Prix and Hakkinen drove through the field from 14th to a superb second place in what was an outstanding race of changing conditions which saw much overtaking and intense racing in track conditions which varied from dry, to torrential rain and then back to patchy damp.

Coulthard, who had qualified fourth on a track that was almost flooded, took the lead from Rubens Barrichello's Stewart on the sixth lap, after having overtaken Olivier Panis and Jean Alesi. He led by 7.6sec by the end of the ninth lap.

Disappointingly, he then stopped on the circuit on lap ten to retire with an electrical power failure. It seemed as though his bitter luck would never take a turn for the better.

Mika climbed through the field, pulling up from eighth by the end of the second lap to fourth on lap ten. Between laps 25 and 35 the safety car was deployed as a heavy rain shower drenched the circuit by which time Mika was right behind Barrichello's leading Stewart. Mika made his first stop during the safety car period, resuming in second place.

On lap 38 Mika, trying to overtake Barrichello for the lead, spun at the Adelaide hairpin and dropped back to seventh, but climbed back through the field to retake second place on lap 57. Three laps later he went back into the lead then made a second refuelling stop in 7.7sec on lap 65, resuming to finish second behind Frentzen's Jordan.

'It was great fun,' said Mika. 'So much happened and I really enjoyed myself. I felt very comfortable with the car and that meant I was able to push for 80 per cent throughout the whole race under all the varying conditions.'

Coulthard only had to wait another fortnight for his first victory of the season. To his delight he won before a

1999 wasn't an easy season for McLaren, what with repeated glitches from man and machine. It was Hakkinen's turn for disaster at Silverstone, and (inset) the Italian GP saw him overwhelmed with frustration when he spun out of the lead after mistakenly selecting first gear. (Formula One Pictures)

sell-out 90,000 crowd at Silverstone. It was not only his first win on home turf, but the first since Imola the year before, and the relief was palpable: 'Just fantastic, the best feeling I have had in my career!' Now it was Hakkinen's turn to suffer calamity. His car was withdrawn from the race on lap 35 after problems with his left rear wheel securing mechanism which had earlier seen the car dramatically shed that rim and tyre out on the circuit.

The race was marred by a first lap accident which removed Michael Schumacher from the championship equation with a broken right leg. On the restart, Hakkinen dominated until his problems intervened after which Coulthard ran home a narrow, but decisive winner over Irvine's Ferrari.

Hakkinen now had 40 points with Schumacher tying with Irvine on 32, Coulthard on 22. Things had definitely taken a turn for the better. Very briefly.

The Austrian Grand Prix produced the lowest moment of Coulthard's F1 career. Barely 20 seconds after the start the Scot wiped out the golden memories of his British victory by shunting team-mate Hakkinen off the road on the second corner of the race.

It was every driver's nightmare, but amazingly things could only get worse as Coulthard was then beaten into second place by Eddie Irvine, rising to the occasion as Ferrari team leader in the absence of Schumacher.

'It was absolutely my ultimate nightmare scenario,' said Coulthard. 'I went off line and considered trying to pass Mika into the first corner, but dropped back again, then, into turn two, I totally misjudged things.

'I broke a front wing endplate in the impact, but that didn't matter. I had a nightmare race and then coming out behind Eddie at the pit stops brought an awful end to an awful day.'

After the rostrum ceremony, Coulthard and Hakkinen, who had driven brilliantly to finish third after resuming last, disappeared into the motorhome with team chief Ron Dennis and Mercedes motorsport director Norbert Haug. Coulthard apologised to Hakkinen for his error, the World Champion accepted graciously and the two men agreed to put the incident behind them.

Amazingly, things could only get worse for Hakkinen at Hockenheim. He suffered a 195mph tyre failure which pitched him into a tyre barrier and out of the German Grand Prix with the same dreadful suddenness that Michael Schumacher had experienced at Silverstone. The accident came on lap 26 after he had already been delayed by a problem with the refuelling rig during his sole scheduled pit stop two laps earlier. He resumed fourth, quickly picked off Frentzen and was hunting down the Ferraris when his McLaren snapped out of control. The Finn was extremely fortunate not to have smashed into the concrete wall on the right of the circuit and there was little in the way of discernible retardation as the McLaren pirouetted wildly on the tarmac and then skated across the top of the gravel bed.

Irvine won again, thanks to Ferrari team orders which put him ahead of Schumacher's stand-in Mika Salo. The Irishman now had 52 points to Hakkinen's 44; Coulthard 30. But then the Italian team's mid-summer boost was dramatically undermined when Hakkinen totally dominated the Hungarian Grand Prix with Coulthard taking second after pressuring Irvine into a driving error towards the finish.

This gave Hakkinen 54 points to Irvine's 56, but Coulthard was now entering the World Championship equation as a challenger in his own right on 36 points.

A fortnight later, Ron Dennis was left vigorously defending his team tactics after Coulthard stormed to a decisive victory in the Belgian Grand Prix at Spa, a race which began with a controversial first corner incident when the team-mates collided.

Hakkinen had qualified on pole position for the tenth time out of 11 races this season, but was slow off the mark after making a slight false start. Coulthard accelerated away down the outside from second place on the grid, then turned into the tight right-hand La Source hairpin where he inadvertently bumped his team-mate's car.

'There has been criticism from some sections of the media when we re-signed David,' said Dennis robustly, 'and now he drives a superb race and there is criticism of our team tactics. The incident was a close call, but David was clearly ahead before the braking point. Any change in the end position would have cost us our long established reputation for dealing totally even handed with our drivers.'

Many F1 insiders took the view that this was all very well, but felt that Dennis risked his drivers racing each other out of the World Championship stakes with only four races left to run.

They suggested that McLaren might live to regret not imposing team orders if Hakkinen, who admitted that he settled for second place at Spa after the first corner episode, should fail to retain his title by a single point.

That view was enhanced after the Italian Grand Prix where Hakkinen, dominant from the start, spun out of the lead in what was his second major driving error of the year. His own mistakes had cost him 20 points, but preparation, mechanical and strategic problems had cost him another 26 points as well, so by the time Heinz-Harald Frentzen crossed the line to win at Monza for Jordan it was hardly surprising that Mika had been seen crouching by the trackside in tears before walking back to the paddock. Coulthard finished fifth.

What had been a slight crisis was now turning into a full-blown panic as McLaren again threw away a possible victory in the European Grand Prix at Nurburgring. A strategically disastrous early switch to wet weather rubber during a fleeting rain shower saw Mika drop to fifth place in a race from which Coulthard slid out of the lead and into a tyre barrier, wiping out his own championship hopes once and for all.

Mika thus went into the penulti-mate championship round at Kuala Lumpur's spectacular new Sepang circuit with 62 points to Irvine's 60.

This was the race marked by Michael Schumacher after a 14 week break since the Silverstone accident. He helped Irvine to win after some brilliantly orchestrated team tactics.

Twice Schumacher gifted the lead to Irvine and spent much of the afternoon keeping Hakkinen boxed up in third place all the way to the chequered flag.

'It was the hardest race of my life,' said the demoralised Finn. 'I was flat out all the way. Ferrari had brilliant tactics and I don't really blame them. I spent most of the race behind Michael but could not get past him. The reason for that was that I had to drive very cautiously as I did not want to get caught out by his inconsistent driving patterns. He was lifting in high speed corners and fluctuating his speed, so I had to be careful not to run into him.'

Hakkinen was the only driver on the grid to opt for the harder of the two Bridgestone tyre compounds in the interests of durability in the sweltering conditions. With that in mind, and the fact that he spent so much time being slowed by Schumacher, many observers felt it was amazing that McLaren did not switch him to the same one stop refuelling strategy to that used by Ferrari for Schumacher.

That would have at least enabled him to keep the pressure on the Ferrari team leader right to the chequered flag instead of losing out with a second refuelling stop with only nine laps to go. This dropped Hakkinen behind Herbert's Stewart-Ford and it was only when the Englishman made a slight mistake four laps from the end that he was able to get back into third place.

Then came some devastating news for the Ferrari team. It came less than two hours after Irvine had celebrated the fact that he would be going into the final race of the season at Suzuka four points ahead of Hakkinen and with a strong chance of becoming Maranello's first World Champion driver for 20 years. At post-race scrutineering the Ferraris were found to have infringed the bodywork rules by having aerodynamic deflectors on the side of the chassis – popularly known as bargeboards – which infringed the permitted dimensions. The stewards decided that the Ferraris had broken the rules and therefore had to be disqualified from the race subject to appeal.

Six days later an FIA appeal court hearing reinstated the Ferraris to their one-two success, relegating Hakkinen to third place, and creating a situation where he went into the final race four points behind Irvine. The Ferraris were reinstated because the FIA conceded that there might have been a mistake in measuring the dimensions of the bargeboards concerned. In the end, the court judged, the bargeboard dimensions fell within the 5mm plus-or-minus tolerance permitted by the technical regulations.

Although FIA President Max Mosley hailed the decision as proof of the independence and fair-mindedness of the FIA appeals procedure, it came as no surprise that the McLaren management felt otherwise.

Ron Dennis said: 'I believe, along with probably every technical director in Formula 1, that the manufacturing tolerance referred to under the [relevant article of the] Technical Regulations has no bearing on any aspect of the car other than the vertical flatness of the horizontal surfaces that form the underside of the vehicle'.

The defending Champion now had it all to do at Suzuka.

Chapter 1

Bruce McLaren
and his legacy

The McLaren team's history spans a period in motor racing history characterised by maximum growth and expansion. When Bruce McLaren founded the team in 1966 his character and personality provided the driving force behind a small company in which everybody was on first-name terms. Today's TAG McLaren empire has a workforce of almost 800 in the Woking area and is one of the biggest employers in that region.

Bruce McLaren's move into the role of team owner in 1964 came largely through force of circumstances. For the five years since he arrived from New Zealand, he had been driving for the British Cooper Formula 1 team and now wanted to contest the Tasman Championship, a prestigious series of single-seater races in Australia and his native country over the winter of 1963/64.

He discussed the matter with his employers, John Cooper and his auto-

cratic father Charles. Shrewdly, McLaren could see that this series would not be a pushover, but Charles Cooper vetoed his suggestion that they develop special cars for this Antipodean adventure. In his view, the existing 1.5-litre Coventry Climax-engined F1 cars would be good enough to do the job.

Yet McLaren wasn't inclined to take no for an answer. This event provided the catalyst that prompted him to set up a business of his own. Bruce McLaren Motor Racing was established and invested in the development of a couple of specially modified Cooper chassis fitted with the more powerful 2.5-litre Climax FPF four-cylinder engines.

In terms of pure result, the Tasman adventure was a success. Bruce won the Championship, but the team was touched by tragedy when his talented young American team-mate Timmy Mayer was killed practising for the final round of the series in Longford,

Tasmania. It was a bitter blow, for young Mayer was due to join Bruce in the Cooper F1 works team for 1964.

Bruce McLaren was born in Auckland on 30 August 1937. From an early age he was noted for a sunny and easy-going disposition that would later permeate his entire racing team. Despite being afflicted dreadfully in his youth by Perthes disease, a potentially debilitating hip condition that effectively kept him bedridden for much of the time between the ages of 9 and 12, young McLaren made a complete recovery to emerge as one of his country's most famous international sportsmen.

There was motor racing blood in Bruce's family from the start. Les McLaren, his father, rebuilt an Austin Seven Ulster for circuit racing in 1951 when his son was barely 14. Almost as soon as he could drive, Bruce began to immerse himself in motorsport, eventually progressing to the point where he acquired the centre-seat 'bob-tailed' 2-litre Cooper in which Jack Brabham had made his F1 debut in the 1955 British Grand Prix at Aintree.

Acquiring this car proved to be a crucial turning point in McLaren's sporting career because it brought him in touch with the taciturn Australian driver who would go on to win the 1959 and 1960 World Championships with a Cooper and a third title in a Brabham in 1966, the only driver to have won the title in a car of his own make. Jack was dour and canny, but willingly entered into correspondence with the young McLaren as he came to grips with the 'bob-tail' back in New Zealand.

Eventually Brabham arranged to take out a couple of single-seater Coopers for the early 1958 Tasman Championship and Bruce was nominated to drive the second car. The young lad from Auckland was on his way.

As a result of his efforts at the wheel of this car, Bruce became the first recipient of an award from the New Zealand International Grand Prix Association of a trip to Europe and an award to cover his expenses during the forthcoming racing season. The Cooper was duly transported to Sydney where it was loaded on the Orient Line steamer *Orantes* for the six-week trip to Britain.

In order to be ready for the start of the 1958 European season, Bruce had to fly ahead of his own car and race a Formula 2 car provided by the Cooper team in his debut race, the Aintree 200 at the Liverpool circuit that existed cheek-by-jowl with the famous Grand National horse-racing track. A succession of promising outings followed in motor racing's international second division, as a result of which Bruce McLaren gained promotion to the Cooper Grand Prix team at the start of 1959.

Throughout his packed, versatile and relatively brief professional racing career in Europe, which, let's remember, lasted only 12 seasons from his race debut to his tragic death two months short of his 33rd birthday, Bruce McLaren built himself a reputation as one of the most solid performers in Grand Prix racing. Not a natural pacesetter, perhaps, but consistent, reliable and – most importantly – a driver with a shrewd grasp of F1's technical dimension. In that respect one could argue that he was almost ahead of his time.

Professional motor racing was undergoing a complex process of evolution in the 1960s. There had always been accomplished engineers in F1's intensely competitive front line, but the sport's administrative establishment was deeply conservative. When McLaren arrived in Europe it would be another ten years before Colin Chapman's Team Lotus heralded in a new commercial era with the arrival of sponsorship from the Gold Leaf cigarette brand.

This was an issue that made quite an impact on Teddy Mayer, Timmy's elder brother, who joined McLaren in 1964 to help bring a degree of semi-professional management to the team's structure.

Mayer, who'd abandoned a career as a lawyer in order to throw in his lot with Bruce, was taken aback with just what an old-school-tie atmosphere prevailed on the British motor racing scene. 'You've got to remember that there were virtually none of the outside commercial sponsors we know today,' he said.

'Virtually all the sponsorship came from oil and tyre companies, and most of the negotiations were carried out via the old pals act. It was as if you waved a mystic wand and the finance appeared.'

Bruce finished sixth in the 1959 World Championship, scoring his maiden F1 win in the final round of the contest, the United States Grand Prix on the Sebring airfield circuit in Florida. The following season opened on a correspondingly upbeat note with victory in the Argentine Grand Prix at Buenos Aires. He went on to finish second in the 1960 World Championship behind team leader Jack Brabham, but would not win again until the 1962 Monaco Grand Prix.

As Cooper's F1 star steadily waned during the early 1960s, so that of Bruce McLaren shone ever more brightly. In 1964 his team purchased the central-seater Cooper-based sports car that American driver Roger Penske had used to win the previous year's important Guards Trophy sports car race at the August Bank Holiday Brands Hatch international meeting.

When Penske raced it the car had been fitted with a Coventry Climax

The man whose name the team still carries to this day, Bruce McLaren. (Phipps Photographic)

four-cylinder engine, but Bruce and his crew installed a more powerful Oldsmobile V8. It proved to be the forerunner of an ever-more-successful generation of rumbling McLaren sports racers powered by big US V8 engines that would dominate the emergent – and very lucrative – North American Can-Am sports car championship for the rest of the decade.

Bruce wanted to go Grand Prix racing with his own car. He could see that Cooper was becoming less and less competitive. Charles Cooper had died late in 1964 and John had been badly injured in a road accident in a twin-engined Mini Cooper special during that same year. The team was clearly on the skids and John would later sell control to the Chipstead Motor Group prior to running Maserati V12 engines for the new 3-litre Formula 1 regulations that came into effect at the start of the 1966 season.

This development would not affect Bruce McLaren, who would decide to go it alone. In 1965 he employed a young designer called Robin Herd to build the prototype single-seater McLaren M2A, which would lay the team's Grand Prix foundations.

In retrospect, the M2A came to be regarded as an over-complex machine from a structural standpoint. The highly qualified Herd had been attracted to the structural rigidity, which would come from using aerospace materials, in this case a composite laminate of special aluminium sheet bonded over a sandwich filling of balsawood. The material was known as Mallite and had originally been developed for internal panelling in the aviation industry. It was light, torsionally rigid, but quite complicated to repair in the event of an accident.

The new car was powered initially by a 4.5-litre Oldsmobile V8 prepared by engine specialists Traco Engineering and was employed as a development vehicle for Firestone's F1 tyres, which would make their Grand Prix debut with the arrival of the new 3-litre Formula 1 the following year.

McLaren finished his Cooper career at the end of 1965 with a disappointing, but not entirely unexpected, eighth place in the Drivers' World Championship. His best result had been a third in Belgium backed up by three fifth places in the South African, Monaco and Italian races. Yet the future looked bright and challenging.

Just before Christmas 1965 the first definite McLaren M2B Formula 1 car was unveiled at the McLaren team's headquarters at Colnbrook, near London Airport. The car was powered by a pushrod Indianapolis V8 engine that had been reduced from 4.2 to 3 litres at Traco's Californian workshops. This linered-down engine was a promising first step, but would not ultimately provide McLaren with a realistic long-term answer to his needs for a seriously competitive F1 power unit.

The McLaren M2B made its debut in Bruce's hands in the 1966 Monaco Grand Prix, where it arrived in distinctive white livery with a broad green stripe rather than the darkish red livery in which the team's sports cars had previously raced. The reason for this paint job was that McLaren's car was doubling as of one of the fictional

'Yamura' F1 cars in Hollywood director John Frankenheimer's film *Grand Prix*, which was being shot during the 1966 World Championship season.

The Ford V8 engine transmitted its reputed 300bhp power output through a rather basic four-speed ZF gearbox, and it didn't take long for Bruce to conclude that a lot more development work would be required if his F1 effort was going to be regarded as anything more than a passing joke.

The McLaren-Ford F1 debut ended when an oil pipe union came undone in the nose section, dousing lubricant all over Bruce's feet and the track surface. The New Zealander switched off the engine before the engine broke.

In truth, this had been a disastrous F1 debut and the Ford V8 was withdrawn for further evaluation and improvement. That left McLaren casting around for a replacement engine, which came from the unlikely direction of Italy in the form of Count Volpi's Serenissima company. They had available a sports-car-based 3-litre V8 that had been produced by Alberto Massimino, the man who had designed some of the very earliest Ferraris, and which was now being developed by Stirling Moss's former F1 mechanic Alf Francis.

Unfortunately the Serenissima V8 produced only about 260bhp, but it was better than leaving the McLaren silent on the Colnbrook factory floor; it was duly installed for the Belgian Grand Prix at Spa-Francorchamps. First experience of the Italian engine proved to be substantially worse than the Ford outing at Monaco. Once coaxed into running on all cylinders, it ran its main bearings inside a lap and had to be withdrawn from the race.

The McLaren-Serenissima made its next F1 appearance in the British Grand Prix at Brands Hatch, where Bruce ran in the top six during the early stages, finally finishing sixth to

For many years Bruce was a stalwart member of the works Cooper F1 team. Here he is on his way to victory in the 1962 Monaco Grand Prix, Cooper's last success under the 1.5-litre F1 regulations. (Phipps Photographic)

score the marque's first World Championship point. It was certainly the start of something big.

However, it would be some considerable time before McLaren's race-winning F1 provenance would slip into a sharper focus. The first few years of the new 3-litre Formula 1 were colourful and ever-changing as teams decided which engines would be the most suitable for their purpose through a process of trial and error. The Indy-based Ford V8 powered Bruce to a fifth-place finish at Watkins Glen in the United States Grand Prix, then failed again in Mexico City. That was the end of that particular project.

McLaren was very busy as a professional driver at this stage in his career, not only with his own fast-expanding Can-Am programme but also with Ford's Le Mans project. Having won Le Mans with his protégé Chris Amon in 1966, he finished a strong fourth in 1967. That season also marked the start of the new 1.6-litre Formula 2 regulations, and the McLaren squad produced the neat little aluminium 'bathtub'-chassis M4A contender, which was aimed at getting a share of the customer F2 market hitherto dominated variously by rivals Lotus and Brabham.

The M4A turned out to be no commercial success, but a specially uprated version of the car was fitted with a 2.1-litre Tasman BRM engine and ballasted up to the F1 weight limit as a temporary expedient for Bruce to drive in Grands Prix early in the 1967 season. He finished a fine fourth at Monaco after which, pending the arrival of the new 3-litre BRM V12 engine to the fully fledged M5A Grand Prix car, the New Zealander was invited to drive Dan Gurney's second Eagle-Weslake in the French, British and German Grands Prix.

The BRM V12 was claimed to produce 370bhp at 9,750rpm, perhaps a rather optimistic assessment on the part of the proud engineering force at the engine-maker's Lincolnshire headquarters. It drove through a Hewland

The orange-painted 1968 McLaren-Cosworth M7A was one of the most handsome Grand Prix cars of its era. Bruce, pictured here, used it to win that year's Race of Champions and Belgian Grand Prix. (Phipps Photographic)

DG five-speed gearbox and was rushed out to the Mosport Park circuit near Toronto for the Canadian Grand Prix after nothing more than a 30-lap shakedown test at Goodwood.

Thirty years ago, the notion of piling thousands of testing miles on to a new car even before the World Championship season began was just not part of the equation. F1 budgets, technical facilities and staffing levels all contributed to what was very much a hand-to-mouth existence in motor racing's premier international formula. Any pre-race testing at all was considered something of a bonus.

The BRM V12 engine proved to be a little longer than expected and some of its accessories projected into the cockpit. Reflecting on this slight design glitch from a distance of 32 years, a week after Mika Hakkinen took the McLaren-Mercedes MP4/14 to its maiden Grand Prix victory in Brazil, this is almost inconceivable.

By 1999 terms of technical reference, such Stone Age mistakes simply could not happen. Ilmor, manufacturers of the Mercedes F1 engines, would by this stage be supplying McLaren with dummy engines of such pin-sharp dimensional accuracy that the entire car could be constructed around them, the engineers concerned certain in the knowledge that when the definitive engine eventually arrived, it would fit

the new chassis like the proverbial glove.

The McLaren M5A ran well enough in the Canadian Grand Prix and on a drying track surged into the lead after an earlier spin. One of the accessories that had been removed in the interests of packaging after the Goodwood test had been the alternator; this was a crucial omission, as Bruce was to realise when the McLaren-BRM began to misfire. Without the alternator the battery was not being charged, which meant that he had to come into the pits for a fresh battery to be fitted. He finished seventh, but his co-director Teddy Mayer would still shudder at the very mention of that missing alternator more than two decades later…

As he braked hard to escape, more leaked fuel fed the inferno

---

Bruce qualified the M5A third fastest at Monza for the Italian Grand Prix where something of a rumpus occurred over the car's red livery, albeit with a silver stripe edged in green in acknowledgement of Bruce's New Zealand nationality. There were remarks to the effect that it was running in the wrong colours – not British Racing Green, which would technically have been correct – but with Ferrari off the pace the Monza organisers adjusted the grid order from '2 by 2' to '3–2–3', which at least put the red McLaren on the front row.

Daft, really, to imagine that any serious Italian racing fan might have thought the M5A was one of theirs!

All this was muscle-flexing, of course, by the standards of what McLaren's team would achieve in F1 when it seriously got into its stride. There was no point in continuing with the BRM V12 even in the unlikely event that it did produce 340bhp. The 1967 Dutch Grand Prix at Zandvoort saw Jim Clark win commandingly with the new Cosworth-Ford DFV-engined Lotus 49 and that all-new V8 had effectively transformed every other F1 power unit to junk status at a stroke.

For 1968 it would be possible to buy the DFVs for £7,500 apiece. McLaren wrote out a cheque for £37,500 – a not inconsiderable sum – and took delivery of five DFVs. Thanks to financial support from Gulf Oil and Goodyear he was in a position to make such an investment and he also signed his fellow Kiwi Denis Hulme, who'd just clinched the 1967 World Championship in a Brabham, to drive the other car. Meanwhile, Robin Herd was designing one of the most visually attractive Grand Prix cars of all time, the elegant McLaren M7A.

This time Herd opted for a more conventional aluminium chassis rather than the Mallite employed for the M2A. However, he had hardly finished work on the concept when he announced that he was leaving to join Cosworth to design its proposed four-wheel-drive Formula 1 car. McLaren was very hurt over this, taking it as a personal slight, although close colleagues noted that it was exactly the same sort of rejection felt by Charles and John Cooper when Jack Brabham left their team at the end of 1961, which Bruce had been unable to understand.

With its bright orange livery and sleek profile, the M7A made is debut in the 1968 Brands Hatch Race of Champions, one of the traditional non-title 'warm-up' races that preceded the main events of the Grand Prix season. Bruce started from pole and won convincingly, his first F1 win since triumphing for Cooper at Monaco six years earlier.

The following month the M7As were out again for the Silverstone International Trophy race, where this time Hulme won ahead of his boss to post the new car's second straight win. Denny kept ahead despite a stone thrown up from the rear wheels of Mika Spence's BRM, knocking the lens out of his goggles and giving him a nasty bash on the head for good measure.

Subsequently Bruce's M7A would be equipped with pannier tanks extending out between the front and rear wheels. As Teddy Mayer recalled, this was effectively designed as a practical test of Bruce's theory that by spreading the fuel load widely across the car its handling would be improved. 'It was one of his theories which, once he became convinced of, he would pursue to the bitter end,' he said.

Unfortunately the pannier-tanked M7A was crashed badly by Bruce at Monaco and he used a regular-spec, but newly built, chassis to win the Belgian Grand Prix at Spa-Francorchamps after Jackie Stewart's dominant Tyrrell Matra had to make a late-race stop to top up with extra fuel.

The M7As continued through the 1968 season as consistent points scorers, but Hulme also won the Italian Grand Prix at Monza and headed Bruce home for a team 1–2 grand slam in the Canadian GP at the St Jovite circuit near Montreal. Denny kept open his mathematical chance of retaining the title crown right through to the final race in Mexico City, although in reality he was a rank outsider. Unfortunately he crashed in the race and it was Graham Hill who emerged as World Champion.

The 1969 Formula 1 season was highlighted by a spate of four-wheel-drive cars, and McLaren didn't want to be left off the bandwagon already occupied by Lotus, Matra and Cosworth. Yet it proved a frustrating blind alley for all concerned.

Designed by the late Jo Marquart, the first of the new four-wheel-drive M9As appeared at Silverstone for the British Grand Prix in the hands of Derek Bell. It had already undergone tests in the hands of Bruce and Denny, but, despite a barrage of encouraging reports in the media, by the time the team arrived at Silverstone it was clear that they were barking up the wrong tree.

Bruce himself coined perhaps the most apt description of the four-wheel-driving sensation; driving the M9A was like 'trying to write your signature with somebody jogging your elbow' and after those preliminary trials he looked glum and said 'Why bother?' to his team.

On the third lap of the British

Grand Prix Bell spun the McLaren at Becketts corner, then retired to the pits after a rear suspension upright broke at Abbey curve. That was the last the public ever saw of the M9A as Bruce quietly forgot the project.

'It was just such an effort to drive,' recalled Hulme years later. 'It had a huge damper on the steering to cut out the kick-back, but it was super-heavy going into the corners. It was intended to be quicker out of the corners, but it wasn't. And the reason for that was that it was much slower in, if you follow me.'

The team reverted to reliance on the M7C, a development of the previous year's car, and Denny scored the team's sole win of the season in the Mexican Grand Prix, setting a blistering pace thanks to Goodyear's latest tyre developments. Bruce finished the season third in the Drivers' Championship with Hulme sixth and the team taking fourth place in the battle for the Constructors' title.

For the 1970 season McLaren produced an all-new two-wheel-drive Formula 1 chassis, the M14A. The team continued to use Cosworth-Ford V8 engines, although a variation of the old M7 chassis was built up to accommodate Alfa Romeo's sports car V8, enabling the Italian company to gain a low-key presence in the Formula 1 arena.

Then came disaster. Hulme was testing one of the new McLaren M15s at Indianapolis when he noticed what looked like water droplets coursing down the windscreen of the car as he rocketed down towards turn one at the famous US speedway. When he went on to the brakes for the corner, methanol fuel gushed out from a flapping filler on the right hand side of the tank and the whole car ignited in a wall of flame.

All Hulme knew was the searing heat. As he braked hard to escape, more leaking fuel fed the inferno. The rugged Kiwi eventually managed to abandon his machine at something just below 70mph. But his hands were terribly burned and Bruce was desperately concerned for his condition. It was an episode that underlined just how close the two friends really were.

Yet there was worse, by far, to come. The team went to Goodwood on 2 June for Peter Gethin to try his hand at the wheel of an M14A in preparation for the Belgian Grand Prix, where he would stand in for the injured Hulme, while Bruce himself would check out the new M8D Can Am contender.

Goodwood may have been closed for racing since 1966, but it remained a worthwhile circuit on which to test. Just after 12.20pm on that sunny summer's day, where a generation earlier Spitfires and Hurricanes would have taken off from what was the former Westhampnett RAF base, Bruce McLaren accelerated out towards the Lavant straight as he had done so many times before.

Tragically, a securing pin was missing from part of the M8D Can Am car's rear bodywork. As the speed built up dramatically, the engine cover and rear wing were torn from the car. It careered out of control and slammed broadside into an earth wall protecting a long-abandoned marshals' post. Bruce McLaren was killed instantly.

Chapter 2

Survival and retrenchment

It would have been quite understandable if the story of the McLaren marque had finished there and then on that summer's afternoon in 1970. But that reckoned without the determination of Teddy Mayer and his co-directors Phil Kerr and Tyler Alexander. They rightly judged that the company had developed a momentum of its own. Bruce might have been the king-pin, but now they determined to continue the work he had started and inspired.

Everybody concerned dug deep into their own personal resources to lift the team's spirits. Hulme, the skin on his fingers still painfully thin and vulnerable, forced himself back into the cockpit of a Grand Prix car long before he was really ready. In an effort to boost the team's fortunes, veteran Dan Gurney was signed up to drive in a handful of races. Yet Gurney, for whose Eagle team Bruce himself had driven only three summers before, was quite clearly past his best. In what was

regarded at the time as an admirable display of honest self-assessment, Dan called it a day after just three races.

'Dan was a great guy to work with, enormous fun,' recalled Teddy Mayer, 'but, God, could he fiddle with a car during practice.' The 1970 season passed without a race victory, for the Marquart-designed M14 was not a great chassis. The following year the Australian designer Ralf Bellamy took charge of the design office and produced the very promising M19, which featured an interesting rising rate suspension system.

On its debut in the 1971 South African Grand Prix at Kyalami Hulme was in cracking form and thrust the new McLaren confidently into the lead, fending off a strong challenge from Mario Andretti's Ferrari. Just when it looked as though victory was in the bag, a bolt fell out of the M19A's suspension, Denny slowed dramatically and Mario cruised by to score his maiden F1 victory. The frustrated Hulme trailed home sixth.

It was a bad day indeed, but things didn't get much better than that as the season unfolded. Mid-season Peter Gethin left the team and moved to BRM, and Peter Revson, the American driver who'd been an old pal of Teddy Mayer and Tyler Alexander back in the early 1960s, joined as Denny's running mate the following year.

The handsome American was a member of the Revlon cosmetics family. Wealthy and charming, he was determined to carve his own furrow. He drove for the McLaren squad – ironically now sponsored by the British Yardley cosmetics company – for two years during which he won two Grands Prix, the 1973 British and Canadian.

'I really got along with him well,' recalls Tyler Alexander, who first acted as Revson's mechanic in club races back in the early 1960s and later ran the McLaren IndyCar operation for which the American also drove.

'His relationship with Teddy was something of a cat-and-mouse scenario, but Peter was a neat guy, a great deal of fun. He was pretty tough, but he always rather had the problem of the family behind him. He was trying to do something himself, off his own bat if you like, rather than simply being painted with the Revlon brush.'

In 1972 Hulme would make up for his previous year's Kyalami disappointment by winning the South African Grand Prix. Revson took third at

Brands Hatch followed by a 2–3 finish in the Austrian Grand Prix at Osterreichring.

That season was also highlighted by the team giving an F1 chance to the dynamic 22-year-old South African Jody Scheckter, but the team's real upsurge in F1 form was consolidated the following year with the arrival of the new Gordon Coppuck-designed McLaren M23.

The M23 made its debut at Kyalami in the third race of the season when Hulme used it to maximum effect, claiming the only pole position of his distinguished Grand Prix career. Yet in an uncomfortable echo of his debut outing in the M19 two years earlier, an apparently commanding win was snatched from his grasp by a punctured

Peter Revson at Kyalami in the 1972 South African Grand Prix in one of the team's Yardley-liveried McLaren M19As. (Phipps Photographic)

rear tyre. He could only finish fifth.

For the British Grand Prix at Silverstone a trio of works M23s were fielded with Scheckter guesting in the third car alongside Hulme and Revson. Coming into Woodcote corner at the end of the opening lap, Jody slammed inside Hulme to take fourth place, but was simply carrying far too much speed to make the turn. He ran wide on to the grass, then spun back across the pack and hit the pit wall, triggering an horrific multi-car pile-up that resulted in the race being red-flagged to a halt.

Nine cars were eliminated, including the luckless Italian Andrea de Adamich who was lifted from the wreckage of his Bernie Ecclestone-owned factory Brabham BT42 with a broken right ankle and left leg. Over

an hour later the race was restarted and although Ronnie Peterson's Lotus 72 made much of the early running, after the track surface was brushed by a light rain shower Peter Revson asserted his advantage to win by 3 seconds.

'Revvie' would go on to win the 1973 Canadian Grand Prix, but despite this achievement continued to have a somewhat ambivalent relationship with Teddy Mayer.

'He was something of a funny guy,' recalled Teddy a decade later. 'I'd known him for all those years and formed the impression he had a bit of a chip on his shoulder. He had a very short fuse and I had a few run-ins with him, but by the end of his time at McLaren he was very quick indeed.

'That victory in the British Grand

Prix was really quite impressive. But I remember one big row centred round whether he would run one particular F1 race or go to Pocono to run the Indianapolis car. I had to put my foot down and point out that our sponsor, Gulf Oil, wanted him at Pocono and that was where he was going. So he went to Pocono and absolutely flew...'

By the end of 1973 McLaren found itself in a difficult position, which, at the same time, could be regarded as enviable. The team was entering the third and final year of its sponsorship deal with Yardley, yet with cost inflation spiralling out of control – price inflation in the UK was hovering around the 20 per cent level at this time – Mayer felt that there was no way in which he could turn down an offer from Marlboro and Texaco, which would be worth in excess of £600,000, perhaps four times the level Yardley was investing.

Hunt showed who was boss by taking pole on his first race in the M23

The resultant negotiations proved to be extremely tense and delicate. Eventually a deal was hammered out whereby the team would run two Marlboro/Texaco-backed M23s for the 1972 World Champion Emerson Fittipaldi and Denny Hulme, plus a single Yardley-backed car for the extremely popular former motorcycle ace Mike Hailwood.

'Mike the Bike' only got the 1974 drive after Chris Amon declined the offer, preferring to commit himself instead to an abortive F1 project of his own. But it was Fittipaldi who took the 1974 World Championship crown for a second time, driving the entire season with an astute blend of flair and tactical acuity. He won the Brazilian, Belgian and Canadian Grands Prix and clinched the crown with a fourth-place finish in the final race of the season at Watkins Glen.

Ironically, Jody Scheckter was also in with a mathematical chance of winning the Championship, albeit at the wheel of a Tyrrell-Ford. Despite his obvious speed, McLaren had decided against retaining his services after 1973 on the basis that he might be a little too expensive in terms of damaged cars. As things turned out, Jody drove beautifully in 1974 and won two races for Tyrrell. Three years later the same questionable judgement would see McLaren pass up the opportunity of securing Gilles Villeneuve's services, offering the same line of argument for rejecting him as they had done with Scheckter.

Fittipaldi finished second to Ferrari rising star Niki Lauda in the 1975 World Championship, then, having won five Grands Prix during the course of two seasons, decided to quit in order to join his brother Wilson's fledgling Copersucar operation. It was career suicide, albeit for the best of reasons, and Fittipaldi would never win another Grand Prix in the five remaining seasons behind the wheel of an F1 car.

Yet doors open and doors close. No sooner did Teddy Mayer hear that

Hailwood – one of racing's nice guys

Mike Hailwood drove for the Yardley McLaren team for barely six months in 1974, but is remembered as one of the most popular drivers the team has ever worked with.

One of the greatest motorcycle racers in the history of the sport 'Mike the Bike' first dabbled in F1 during the early 1960s when he drove a private Lotus-BRM 25 for the Parnell Racing organisation. He finished sixth at Monaco in 1964 but concentrated on two-wheeled competition for the next seven years and did not return to F1 until Monza, 1971, where he finished fourth for John Surtees's team.

He drove for Surtees through until the end of 1973 when, seeking more competitive pastures, he switched to McLaren. He finished third in South Africa, fourth in Argentina and Holland and fifth in Brazil. Sadly, he crashed heavily in the German Grand Prix at Nurburgring, badly injuring an ankle in an accident which effectively ended his F1 career at the age of 34.

Genial, kindly and totally without pretence, this millionaire's son could be quite a handful socially when he let his hair down, but there was no doubting Mike Hailwood's totally professional approach towards his chosen sport. His death in 1981, in a road accident which also claimed the life of his young daughter Michelle, left the motor racing community utterly bereft.

Emerson was yesterday's news than he put through a call to the British driver James Hunt, recently made redundant after Hesketh Racing closed its doors as a front-line F1 operation. Hunt had been in the throes of negotiating with Lotus boss Colin Chapman, but both parties were making heavy weather of the talks.

Chapman still clung to the belief that people ought to be honoured to drive for Lotus and that it was better to invest money in the car's technology rather than the driver's retainer. James replied that this was all very well, but he was a professional racer and Lotus was poised on the outer rim of competitiveness. Bottom line was, he needed paying.

Mayer immediately told him to stop talking to anybody until they had time to talk seriously together. The net result was that Teddy got James's signature on a 1976 contract for a reputed £40,000. This was chicken-feed, even by the standards of the age, but for McLaren it would prove one of F1's all-time bargains.

James was partnered by Jochen Mass, the pleasant German driver who had been drafted into the McLaren squad towards the end of 1974 after Mike Hailwood suffered severe ankle injuries when he crashed heavily during the German Grand Prix at Nurburgring. Mass privately believed that he might be in a position to assert an advantage over his incoming rival, but Hunt quickly showed who was boss by qualifying on pole position for his first race in the M23, the Brazilian GP at Interlagos.

In taking on the team leadership, James now found himself pitted directly against his old friend Niki Lauda, whose Ferrari 312T he had beaten into second place to score his maiden Grand Prix win in Holland with the Hesketh 308 in 1975.

On that occasion the race had started in the wet and James perfectly timed his switch to slicks, leaving Lauda running behind him for the second part of the race.

'James drove beautifully,' remembers Lauda, 'and there was understandably a great deal of excitement amongst the British press about his achievement, although, if I am honest, I would have to say that I took things a little easier than I might have done as my main priority that day was to keep scoring points to add to my World Championship tally. Nevertheless, James's success took him through a psychological barrier, which was bad for me.'

Niki won the Championship in 1975, but it soon became clear that he was going to have his work cut out if he was going to retain it in 1976.

'From the moment he got into the McLaren M23, James was predictably quick,' continued the Austrian. 'The 1976 season has now gone down in motor racing history as one of the most remarkable of all time, but I have to confess I still felt very confident about the Ferrari 312T's performance in the opening races of the year.

'I won in Brazil and in South Africa, then again at Belgium and Monaco. But around that time both James and I began to encounter our troubles. I damaged a rib when a tractor rolled over on top of me while I was in the garden of my new home at Hof, near Salzburg. And James won the Spanish Grand Prix for McLaren, beating me in the process, only to be disqualified when his car was found to have a fractionally too wide rear track.'

The McLaren team seriously believed it had got the raw end of the deal in that race on Madrid's Jarama circuit. There was a feeling, which would be compounded again and again during the course of that summer, that Ferrari somehow represented 'The Establishment' and that the sport's governing body were showing a degree of partiality towards the famous Italian team. It was a theme that would emerge regularly over the years, in particular – and with some intensity – since 1996 when Michael Schumacher signed up at Maranello.

Eventually James's race win in Spain was re-instated, which left Ferrari, on this occasion, feeling a bit miffed. Personal tensions began to build between James and Niki, although they were on a pretty mild level compared with some of the internecine strife between rivals that would follow over the ensuing decades. 'We were rivals, but we respected each other totally, whatever the circumstances,' said Niki.

James then won the French Grand Prix at Paul Ricard after both Ferraris encountered engine problems. Then came the controversy of the British Grand Prix at Brands Hatch. Lauda's Ferrari team-mate Clay Regazzoni touched wheels accelerating away from the start into Paddock Bend, then James's McLaren was pitched on to two wheels when he rode over the other Ferrari's wheel.

The race was red flagged to a halt and James eventually took the re-start in his repaired race car, although McLaren initially wheeled out the spare car for him, which was clearly against the rules. Technically he shouldn't have been allowed to take the re-start at all, but it seemed to many onlookers that the race officials were so overwhelmed by the fans' vocal support for James that they relented.

'I suppose I was cast in the role of the villain in their eyes, although I have to confess this didn't really bother me in the slightest,' said Lauda. 'Having said that, in the later years of my career – particularly when I returned after my break to drive a McLaren – I tended to find the British fans extremely hospitable towards me, especially after I won at Brands Hatch in 1982 and 1984.'

Hunt's McLaren M23 stalked Lauda relentlessly after the British Grand Prix was restarted and eventually sliced past into the lead with a bold move going into the Druids hairpin. He would be disqualified from that win later in the season, by which time Lauda was fighting back to health after his Ferrari had been transformed into a fireball when he crashed in the German Grand Prix at Nurburgring.

Lauda hung between life and death for several days and, while his old friend was enormously concerned about his condition, it nevertheless gave Hunt a golden opportunity to close the points gap on the Austrian. James won the restarted German GP –

James Hunt and Niki Lauda were the closest of friends throughout their racing careers – and both won World Championships for McLaren. (Formula One Pictures)

before the extent of Niki's injuries were fully appreciated – but by the time the next two races came round it was happily clear that the Austrian was well on the road to staging a remarkable recovery.

'By the time I got back in the cockpit for the Italian Grand Prix at Monza, I was only 2 points ahead of James at the head of the World Championship table,' said Lauda. 'I finished fourth there and James didn't score, so now I was 5 points ahead with three races to go. Then James got disqualified from the British Grand Prix, promoting me to the win, and he went into the Canadian Grand Prix 17 points behind.

'People have often asked me whether I felt sympathy for James on this, and I suppose I would have to say no, even though there was quite a bit of tension between the McLaren and Ferrari teams. We were locked in pretty fierce competition for that Championship, but we were both professionals and didn't allow our personal friendship to get in the way of that rivalry. But I would say that James drove the last few races of 1976 – and the first of 1977 – about as well as at any other time in his career.'

At the same time, McLaren had really piled on the development of the M23, which, although not quite as powerful as the Ferrari, was certainly a tried and tested car with a well-proven competition record behind it. Lauda paid the price for Ferrari's lack of development with a distant eighth in the Canadian and third in the US Grand Prix, both won by Hunt.

Then came the electrifying finale to a quite remarkable season. In the Japanese Grand Prix at Mount Fuji Lauda pulled out of the race on the second lap, convinced that driving in such torrential rain was absolute lunacy.

Some people said that Niki had taken a calculated gamble that James wouldn't finish the race, but that was unfair. Niki had nothing to prove after that incredible return to the cockpit. For his part, Hunt looked as though he had the race in the bag only to be sent scurrying into the pits to change a deflated tyre. He resumed the chase, throwing caution to the wind and storming back to third place – enough to give him the Championship crown by a single point ahead of Lauda.

There was still an element of sportsmanship to the Grand Prix business in those days. Hunt made some very public remarks that were supportive of Lauda in the weeks immediately after the Japanese Grand Prix at a time when the Austrian was being put through the mill by an unforgiving Italian press after being seen to throw in the towel and lose the title at the final gasp.

In retrospect, there seems no doubt that Hunt was at his personal peak in 1976 and 1977. During the summer of 1976 McLaren had produced a new car, the M26, essentially an M23 uprated round a lighter, stronger and stiffer aluminium honeycomb chassis, but it did not become the team's regular kit until well into the following season, such was the sustained competitiveness of the older car, now in its fourth racing season.

Sadly, McLaren's F1 fortunes began

to drift just as Hunt's driving began to lose its committed edge. One shortcoming might have contributed to the other, but either way the team was certainly being left behind in terms of technology. In retrospect, when one reflects on the 1977/78 seasons it is quite remarkable just how Colin Chapman's Team Lotus wrong-footed the opposition with its wing cars, harnessing the airflow beneath the chassis to create downforce.

Even in 1978 – by which time the Lotus 79 had taken Chapman's team into what was effectively the second chapter of the ground-effect era – McLaren was still relying on the uprated M18. And getting nowhere not very fast.

It seemed as though things could only get worse. James was told by Teddy Mayer that McLaren would not be renewing his contract for 1979. Instead, the great Swedish driver Ronnie Peterson was signed up to replace him. Tragically, 'SuperSwede' died at Monza from injuries sustained in a start-line pile-up in the 1978 Italian GP. McLaren had to cast around for a replacement and opted for John Watson, the pleasant and popular Ulsterman who had previously driven alongside Lauda in the Brabham-Alfa squad.

Gordon Coppuck pencilled his own interpretation of the ground-effect theme, the end result being the McLaren M28. Heavy, slow and aerodynamically flawed, it was totally uncompetitive. A disaster. Teddy Mayer intervened and effectively told his design team to produce a brand new car in time for the British Grand Prix.

'That M28 was ghastly, a disaster,' said Mayer. 'It was ludicrous, quite diabolical. Gordon's track record was not looking too good with the M28 following on behind the M26. I'm afraid we ignored all the crucial design precepts that a car should be as light, agile and compact as possible. And its failure came at a particularly difficult time for the team.

'Interestingly, the M28's uncompetitiveness didn't unduly get on top of Watson. It was so obvious that the car was hopeless that he didn't worry about

Hunt on the rostrum at Silverstone after winning the 1977 British Grand Prix in the new McLaren M26. (Formula One Pictures)

The M23, a quite remarkable racing car

McLaren's M23 was one of the longest-lived Grand Prix cars of its era. Making its debut in the 1973 South African Grand Prix at Kyalami in the hands of Denny Hulme, the car's last outing was with young Brazilian Nelson Piquet, who drove the private B. & S. Fabrications-entered car to ninth place in the Italian Grand Prix at Monza five and a half years later.

The car won 18 World Championship Grands Prix, although in the last two seasons of its career it was displaced as a front-line challenger and spent its time in the hands of privateers, having run its last outing for the factory team in the hands of Gilles Villeneuve in the 1977 British Grand Prix at Silverstone.

The elegant M23, with its side radiators and balanced lines, was Gordon Coppuck's first complete Formula 1 design. It was also one of the first F1 cars tailor-made to the new technical regulations, introduced that season, that required a deformable structure along the side of the chassis to provide added protection to the fuel tanks in the event of a lateral impact.

The M23 inherited the rising rate front suspension from the earlier M19, while conventional rear suspension, with outboard spring/dampers, adjustable top links, reversed lower wishbones and twin radius rods were fitted. The car had a centre fuel cell behind the driver's seat, and the Cosworth Ford DFV V8 engine transmitted its power through a Hewland FG400 transaxle.

During its first season the M23 won three Grands Prix, the first being Hulme's victory in the Swedish Grand Prix at Anderstorp where he snatched the lead from Ronnie Peterson's Lotus 72 in the closing stages. Peter Revson then went on to win at Silverstone and Canada's Mosport Park track, while Hulme started the 1974 season with a lucky win at Buenos Aires after Carlos Reutemann's Brabham BT44 ran out of fuel.

For the 1974 season the M23s were revamped with revised weight distribution achieved by means of a 3-inch spacer between the engine and gearbox, which lengthened the wheelbase. The rear track was also wider, but new team leader Emerson Fittipaldi was not totally convinced about these changes and experimented with different wheelbase lengths as he worked his way to the 1974 World Championship title.

For the start of the 1975 season Fittipaldi appeared in a car with heavily revised front suspension, Gordon Coppuck having taken a leaf out of Brabham's book by adopting a fabricated top rocker arm configuration with pullrod activation of the now semi-inboard spring/damper unit. This was later modified to move the spring/dampers totally inboard again, and a variety of secondary suspension modifications were incorporated progressively over the balance of the season in which Fittipaldi took second place in the Championship.

For 1976 Fittipaldi switched to the Brazilian Copersucar team, which had been established the previous year by his elder brother Wilson. That brought the extrovert, public-school-educated James Hunt into McLaren as number one driver, the Englishman successfully exploiting the M23's continuing development potential to beat Ferrari's Niki Lauda to that year's World Championship.

Into 1977 and there was still precious little indication that the McLaren M23 was at the end of its competitive life. The new M26, introduced mid-season 1976, was proving difficult to sort out and it was not until after Monaco that Hunt abandoned the M23 and switched to the new car. His final race win with the M23 came in the Race of Champions at Brands Hatch, the non-title curtain-raiser to the European season.

American privateer Brett Lunger continued to run an M23 through the summer of 1977 and into 1978 before changing it for an M26. By this time these veteran McLarens were being handed down into the British national scene and Piquet's outing in the M23 at Monza on 10 September rang down the curtain on the front-line career of a quite remarkable racing car.

James Hunt won the 1976 World Championship in the Marlboro McLaren M23 (below) – more than three years after Denny Hulme put the distinctive side-radiatored car on pole position for its debut in the 1973 South African Grand Prix (bottom). (Phipps Photographic)

By the time James Hunt competed in the 1978 British Grand Prix at Brands Hatch, the McLaren M26 had been overtaken technically by the new breed of ground-effect car. (Formula One Pictures)

it. It was later that we had problems, in 1979, when he got his hands on the M29.'

The arrival of the new M29 may have enabled the team briefly to stem the flood tide, but it was clear that it had lost its overall momentum. Nevertheless, there were some bright moments, most notably when Marlboro's Paddy McNally introduced Mayer to a young Alain Prost at Watkins Glen in 1979. A month later the French rising star would be given a test run at Paul Ricard.

As Teddy remembered, 'I watched for ten laps, then ran to my car to get a draft contract from my briefcase.' This young man was clearly very special indeed and launched his F1 career with a sixth place in the 1980 Argentine Grand Prix followed immediately by fifth in Brazil.

Yet even Prost's arrival could not reverse the trend. Marlboro, the team's title sponsor, was also getting nervous and pressing Mayer to get a firm handle on the situation. It was clear that the design capability of the company needed strengthening without delay.

Teddy decided to approach John Barnard with an offer of a job. John, who had worked for McLaren initially back in the early 1970s, had just returned from the US after a successful spell designing the Chaparral IndyCar for Texan racer Jim Hall.

It was the McLaren boss's idea that Barnard could work alongside Gordon Coppuck, but the strong-willed 'JB' wasn't interested in such an alliance. He wanted Teddy to dismiss Coppuck, and Teddy wasn't prepared to do that. The proposed deal came to nothing.

This was a crucial moment. Barnard went off to join Ron Dennis and began sketching out an F1 chassis built out of carbon-fibre composite materials, a revolutionary departure from the aluminium honeycomb that was *de rigeur* at the time. Dennis was hot for F1 after years of running his own Formula 2 teams to a very high standard of preparation.

In 1979 Marlboro had nudged Mayer towards an amalgamation with Dennis's Project Four organisation. The American lawyer declined. By the summer of 1980 the McLaren team's prime sponsor was back explaining its viewpoint in rather more persuasive detail. The bottom line was that if Mayer didn't engineer a deal with Dennis and Barnard, McLaren's sponsorship package would be history.

As a result of this, a new company titled McLaren International came into existence in September 1980. Mayer and Dennis were named as joint Managing Directors, but with Mayer already owning 85 per cent of the original McLaren shareholding, he now became the biggest single shareholder in the new organisation with 45 per cent of its equity. Part of the deal also involved dispensing with Gordon Coppuck's services, a task that pained Mayer considerably as, despite the recent failures, this likeable engineer had contributed so much to the McLaren team effort for more than a decade.

The most unfortunate aspect of the 1980 season came when Alain Prost decided that he was leaving at the end of the year. Contract or no contract, option or no option, he'd decided that the McLaren was suffering too many structural failures. A big shunt at Watkins Glen finally sealed the little Frenchman's resolve. Even if he had to stop racing, he wouldn't continue driving for McLaren.

It was an ironic situation. Alain signed for Renault, where he would stay for three seasons. Then he would return to the revitalised McLaren International enclave and mature into one of the most popular and glitteringly successful stars in its entire history.

Chapter 3

Ron Dennis
takes the helm

In collaboration with John Barnard, Ron Dennis revitalised and invigorated the McLaren team. Dennis was a visionary. He was never what one would describe as a dyed-in-the-wool car enthusiast, but had a fascination for technical matters. And preferably technical excellence.

He started life as a mechanic with the works Cooper Formula 1 team in the summer of 1966. In those days the mechanics in Grand Prix motor racing had quite a tough life. The paddocks were often little more than gravel-strewn fields and the mechanics frequently had to work in the open. At best there was some protection from temporary awnings erected alongside the transporters, but generally work on the cars was conducted in the open.

Ron concedes that he's always been something of an 'old woman' when it comes to cleanliness and order. But he never saw any merit in grubby equipment or personnel. Within half an hour of getting home from the factory after a day's work, Ron would always wash himself down, change into fresh clothes and appear as clean as a new pin. It is a philosophy he has sustained to this day.

After learning the motor racing ropes with Cooper, Ron Dennis switched to the Brabham team for 1968, and by the end of 1970 had been promoted to Chief Mechanic. In fact, for the last two races of that season he was effectively operating as team manager. He was now sufficiently confident to strike out on his own.

For 1971 he established Rondel Racing together with his close friend and colleague Neil Trundle, whom he had met while they were both working for the Brabham squad. The plan was to field a single Formula 2 Brabham BT36, initially loaned from Ron Tauranac who had purchased the Brabham organisation from its founder Jack Brabham after the Australian driver decided to retire at the end of the 1970 season.

The Rondel car was to be driven by up-and-coming Australian Tim Schenken, but this was soon supplemented by a second car for the young Frenchman Bob Wollek. The Rondel cars were absolutely immaculate, Dennis effectively laying down a marker in terms of preparation that would eventually set the tone for McLaren International when it swung into action at the end of the 1980 season.

Dennis remained in Formula 2 for most of the 1970s. In the free-wheeling world of professional motor racing he gained a reputation as an astute professional. There were many who wanted to get into Formula 1 at all costs, but Dennis's enthusiasm for engineering excellence was tempered by a degree of business savvy. He was interested in Formula 1, sure enough, but not at any price. If he was going to do it, he would do it properly.

As things transpired, Dennis would build the firm business base of his Project Four company as the result of an unexpected development. In 1979 BMW introduced its new M1 super-car and Dennis's company was one of several commissioned to prepare a number of these machines for the 'one-make' Procar series that was staged as a series of supporting events at key European Grands Prix that season.

More significantly, Project Four ran its own Marlboro-backed M1 for Niki Lauda in the 1979 series, winning the title. Dennis could see this as a worthwhile springboard to a Formula 1 involvement. And he made it work.

Ron now worked to get a deal together with a top Formula 1 designer. He approached Gordon Murray at

Andrea de Cesaris in the McLaren M29B in the pit lane at Long Beach in 1981, the race that marked the start of the McLaren International era. (Formula One Pictures)

John Watson rounds the hairpin at Montreal during the 1981 Canadian Grand Prix in the carbon-fibre composite McLaren MP4, which he drove to the reconstituted team's first win in that year's British Grand Prix. (Formula One Pictures)

Brabham and Patrick Head at Williams, but both were settled in successful positions and had no interest in moving. He then approached the independent-minded John Barnard, who, Ron later admitted, didn't seem to be terribly interested in his ideas. Not at first glance, anyway.

However, when Dennis made it clear that he envisaged Barnard having an absolutely free hand on the technical side, the two men began to talk seriously. Ron showed the engineer a carbon-fibre composite rear wing from one of the BMW M1 racers. It immediately set JB thinking in terms of manufacturing a completely new Grand Prix chassis from this very advanced material.

Barnard eventually concluded that building a chassis from carbon-fibre composite would have enormous structural benefits. It would combine impact resistance with terrific torsional stiffness, the latter being a significant priority at a time when F1 designers were attempting to control the airflow beneath the car in an effort to generate optimum aerodynamic downforce.

Dennis tried to raise the necessary funding, estimated to be around £80,000. It was not enough, but events were going their way when Marlboro took steps to broker their marriage with McLaren International.

Teaming up with John Barnard was one of the shrewdest moves Ron Dennis would ever make. Their partnership lasted for six years, but during that time it set in stone the McLaren International operational parameters. Both men were perfectionists, sometimes difficult to work for and always uncompromising in their attitudes towards the job in hand.

After McLaren International was established there was a slightly uncertain spell as Barnard finalised the design of his new carbon-fibre composite challenger. An old friend, Steve Nichols, who had worked on the US IndyCar scene, put Barnard in touch with Hercules Aerospace in Salt Lake City, and one afternoon Dennis telephoned to suggest what he had in

mind. Hercules listened with interest and a deal was struck to supply the fledgling Formula 1 team with the necessary carbon-fibre composite materials for the new MP4.

At the launch of the new car much was made of the fact that it was not only stiffer, lighter and safer than a conventional aluminium honeycomb chassis, but also that the number of components used in its construction had been reduced by about 90 per cent. Barnard estimated that around 50 sections of aluminium had been required to complete one of the superseded M29 chassis. Now there were just five main CFC panels on the MP4 in addition to its outer shell.

McLaren's driver line-up for the 1981 season saw the resilient Watson paired with the young Italian Andrea de Cesaris. However, the season was marked by a change in the Formula 1 regulations that saw aerodynamic sliding skirts banned in an effort on the part of the governing body to reduce lap speeds. But pre-season testing raised the McLaren team's hopes and Watson eventually gave the new Cosworth-engined car its race debut in the Argentine Grand Prix, where it ran promisingly just behind the leading bunch before retiring with a severe chassis vibration.

Having been robbed of the side-skirts, the British teams embarked on a programme to enable the cars to run as close to the track surface as possible in

Two perfectionists together

On the face of it, one might conclude that Ron Dennis and John Barnard are two very different personalities. Meet them in 1999 – some 13 years after they parted company as McLaren collaborators – and it may be difficult to see what drew them together in the first place.

Hidden beneath the surface, Dennis has the capacity to laugh at himself and a zany sense of fun. In fact, as those who've attended McLaren end-of-season parties can attest, if anything he's probably a bit too full of beans when he's offstage. But in public these qualities are concealed beneath a cool and calm exterior. He contains his emotions extremely well in the intense environment of the pit lane, but can be uncompromisingly assertive when it comes to business dealings.

Barnard has more of an obvious twinkle in his eye. He is gregarious and chatty, but has quite a formidable reputation for getting his own way. As the Porsche engineers at Weissach discovered during the 1983 season, he would not compromise on the configuration of the new TAG turbo V6. Vee angle, position of ancillary pumps and other equipment, overall dimensional requirements, all were rigorously laid down by the British engineer who was not above getting into ferocious arguments to make a point.

The same applied in his relationship with Dennis. Frequently the two men sparked off each other and there were rumours that one mechanic used to slide off home when the factory at Pool Road, Woking, was rocked by one of these internecine verbals spats, telling the receptionist to give him a bell when the coast was clear.

Yet the Dennis/Barnard partnership worked brilliantly until 1985 when John decided to sell his stake in the company to TAG boss Mansour Ojjeh. At about the same time he and Ron began to drift apart, increasingly at odds with each other over certain aspects of the McLaren corporate structure.

'I sold my shareholding to Mansour because I quite liked the idea of having a nice house and a bit of money,' said an effort to claw back some of the lost advantage. The new rules stipulated a 6cm ground clearance requirement, but the teams initially employed a novel double spring system whereby the suspension would gradually compress under air pressure at high speed, then rise up to be 'legal' when the car entered the pit lane. It was all good knockabout stuff.

Whatever the rules, the McLaren MP4 came on strongly almost from the start. Watson was third in the Spanish Grand Prix at Jarama, second in the French race at Dijon-Prenois, then emerged triumphant in the British Grand Prix at Silverstone, vindicating Ron Dennis who had confidently told Marlboro that the MP4 would win at least one race during its maiden season.

For 1982 there were two more surprises in store. Not only did Dennis manage to lure retired double-World Champion Niki Lauda back into the

Barnard. 'That left Ron with a 40 per cent shareholding, and although I was still Technical Director, our relationship changed subtly because I was now effectively an employee.'

The increasingly uncomfortable situation finally came to a head in August 1986 when Dennis felt that Barnard's negotiations, notably with BMW Motorsport over the possible design of an F1 car for the German company, had gone too far. John agreed that it was time for him to seek pastures new and, while the BMW deal eventually failed to get off the ground, he soon found a position in charge of a new design out-station that he was commissioned to establish for the Ferrari team near Guildford.

'We had achieved everything together that we had set out to do and there was a variety of choices available to myself and John,' reflected Dennis. 'The easy route for both of us, and certainly the easy route for me, would be to have no change. But when faced with all the things that affected that decision to either continue together or not, we decided to split.

'Each's contribution was inaccurately perceived by the other, and I think there was more of an inaccuracy on his side as to what I was contributing in generating finances, and all that sort of thing.'

For his part, Barnard came to agree with this theory, at least in part. 'I think that Ron changed the situation in his own mind,' he pondered. 'A funny, intangible element entered our relationship. I don't think he wanted the situation to change, but it did.

'But I do think, in retrospect, that we both underestimated our partnership. My mistake was thinking that everybody else was doing the same as we were at McLaren. When I eventually went out to other teams, my mouth literally hit the floor. They were not even close in terms of technology. I was dead naive in that respect and sometimes look back with regret over my break with McLaren. Where would we be now if we had stayed together?'

Yet Barnard certainly left a legacy, an impetus, on the technical side of the McLaren team that lasts through to this day – namely a deep conviction that the very best is only just good enough.

cockpit, but he persuaded the TAG high technology group to bankroll the development of a specially commissioned 1.5-litre turbocharged V6 engine from Porsche.

This was a shrewd move by Dennis. He had not *asked* Porsche whether they would support his team through the provision of a Grand Prix engine. Instead, he was in the driving seat from the outset for the whole project. He was the customer who laid down the requirements and footed the bill. Porsche was only too happy to enter into such a commercial agreement, although John Barnard would certainly prove to be a hard taskmaster for the famous German company, which was used to advising other people on the intricacies of engine development.

The TAG turbo V6 would be completely race-ready in 1984 (although it had appeared the previous season), giving Porsche two years to develop and build the engine to Barnard's stringent design specifications. In the meantime, McLaren continued for two more seasons with Lauda and Watson driving Cosworth

Niki Lauda was tempted out of retirement by Ron Dennis at the start of 1982.
(Formula One Pictures)

V8-engined developments of the original MP4 design

Lauda had quit F1 midway through practice for the Canadian Grand Prix in 1979 when he was driving for the Brabham team. He had tired of driving and wanted to spend more time concentrating on his fledgling airline Lauda-air, which he had originally founded in 1978. But by the end of 1981 Dennis correctly judged that the pragmatic Austrian might be ripe for a return to the cockpit. He invited Niki for a test run at Donington Park.

'Once I'd made the decision to come back, the rest was easy,' said Lauda. 'OK, so I had a few fleeting doubts when I did that Donington test for the first time, but it was my own fault. I'd put myself in a new car, on a track I'd never seen before, on radial tyres that I'd never tried before. But the worry soon passed. By the end of the day, I reckoned I could do it.'

Indeed Lauda could. Despite agreeing to a contract that enabled McLaren to extricate itself from the deal after every three races if he didn't perform. 'But then I won Long Beach, the third race of the 1982 season,' recalled Niki with some glee, 'and they came back pressing me to sign a long-term contract for 1983 and 1984.

'So I said, "Fine, but now I want four million dollars, but now you have to pay me for the driving as well. In the past you only agreed to employ me for the publicity." So for two years I had four million dollars, but it all went wrong when we started negotiating for 1985.'

Thus, by the first few months of 1982, Ron Dennis had McLaren

Niki Lauda on the rostrum after winning the 1982 British Grand Prix at Brands Hatch for McLaren, beating Ferrari drivers Didier Pironi and Patrick Tambay. (Formula One Pictures)

International firmly placed on the start of the path to sustained Formula 1 success. Porsche was busy fettling away on the new engine and Lauda went on to add the British Grand Prix to his list of victories, supplemented by John Watson's wins in the Belgian and Detroit Grands Prix.

Watson was every bit as determined a driver as Niki when he was strapped in the cockpit, but outside the car he always seemed more gentle and less assertive. Yet it would fall to the pleasant Ulsterman to score McLaren's only victory of 1983, one that would not only turn out to be the last posted by a Cosworth-engined team car but also the last of his own driving career.

In 1982 John displayed huge deter-mination and overtaking ability when he stormed to victory through the streets of Detroit, and the following year he did it again in similar circum-stances at Long Beach. He qualified 22nd and Niki 23rd, the two drivers frustrated by an apparent dire lack of grip from their Michelin radial tyres.

However, on race day slightly higher track temperatures prevailed and both McLarens flew, John displacing Niki to take the win and head an MP4/1C one-two. John would stay on with the team through to the end of the 1983 season, but his contract would not be renewed for the following season. It marked the end of his Grand Prix career at the age of 37. Yet he always appeared remarkably philosophical

John Watson scored the final Grand Prix victory of his career here at Long Beach in 1983 where he is seen ahead of Andrea de Cesaris's Alfa Romeo and his McLaren team-mate Niki Lauda. The McLarens qualified outside the top 20 only to romp through to a 1–2 success once they got some heat in their tyres. (Formula One Pictures)

about the hand that circumstances had dealt him.

Having failed to win the 1983 World Championship at the wheel of his Renault, Alain Prost was effectively made the fall guy and was fired by the French national car-maker. Ron Dennis suddenly found himself being presented with a gift on a plate at a bargain bucket price. Prost was one of the most brilliant F1 performers and he had nothing to drive. McLaren International snapped him up.

'I had nothing else, and Ron knew it,' conceded the Frenchman. 'It embarrasses me now that I signed for so little, but at the time I didn't care. I was away from Renault, and that was all that mattered.'

Watson recalls how extremely disappointed Dennis had been when Prost originally left McLaren in 1980. 'He knew what was coming in terms of new technology and he couldn't convince Alain of it at that particular time.

'I also think that Ron was talking to everyone in 1983, but as far as I was concerned there were no negotiations with McLaren for 1984. I had a one-year contract for 1983 and, when I got to Kyalami for the last race of the season, the first signs of any discussions came from Marlboro's Paddy McNally. He said, "I suppose we're going to have to talk to you for 1984", and I said, "Sure, any time you like." But that was all there was.

'Then Alain became available. For me it was a hard fact that I had to come to terms with and get on with the rest of my life.'

Chapter 4

The TAG turbo years

TAG – short for Techniques d'Avant Garde – is a well-known name in motor racing circles in the 1990s. Not only is McLaren International now a constituent company within the TAG McLaren Group, but the company is firmly identified within the consumer goods market, the result of having acquired the famous Swiss watchmaker Heuer in 1985.

One of the keys to Heuer's success

One of the early TAG turbo V6s in the McLaren MP4/1E development chassis, Monza, 1983. (Formula One Pictures)

had been its determination to dominate the world of sports timing; back in 1916 the company filed a patent for its 'Micrograph', which was the first device capable of measuring one-hundredths of a second. It was only natural that the TAG Heuer brand should become a sponsor of the McLaren Grand Prix team, and since 1992 it has also been the official time-keeper for the FIA Formula 1 World Championship.

However, TAG's involvement in motor racing originally came as a sponsor of the Williams team in 1979. Techniques d'Avante Garde is a Luxembourg-based holding company established in 1977 by the late Akram Ojjeh, a Franco-Lebanese entrepreneur who may be best known by the general public for brokering the deal for the sale of the SS *France*, the biggest ocean liner in the world, to its current owners who have renamed it the SS *Norway*.

Through the enthusiasm of Akram Ojjeh's two sons, Mansour and Abdulaziz, TAG became co-sponsors of the Williams team in 1980 when it was also closely associated with various Saudi Arabian backers.

However, Ron Dennis approached Mansour Ojjeh at the 1981 Brazilian Grand Prix with a proposal that TAG might like to sponsor the construction of the forthcoming Porsche-built F1 engine that McLaren was commissioning. Delicate negotiations followed, with Ojjeh initially agreeing in principle, but with the proviso that Williams should also have access to supplies of the new engine.

In fairness, this was a scenario that appealed to neither Dennis nor Williams. Both understood the need for exclusivity of engine supply as F1 moved into the highly competitive turbo era, and eventually TAG threw in its lot with Ron Dennis's operation while simultaneously scaling down its sponsorship of the Williams team over the next two seasons. Ironically, Williams then went off to secure a works engine deal with Honda, which, in 1986 and 1987, would result in their toppling the McLaren-TAGs from their World Championship stranglehold.

Barnard had insisted that the engine be as light and compact as possible, the better to maximise its packaging into what he hoped would be the 'ultimate'

Lauda hinted at the McLaren-TAG's promise by setting a competitive pace in the 1983 South African Grand Prix.
(Formula One Pictures)

ground-effect F1 chassis. John was therefore bitterly frustrated when the FIA banned sculpted underbodies from the start of 1983, insisting instead on flat bottoms for all F1 cars from then on.

'The engine specification would have been different if we had been running flat-bottomed rules from the start,' fumed the McLaren designer. Even so, the McLaren-TAG package would still prove to be the class of the contemporary F1 field when it finally made its race debut.

The new 1499cc TAG turbo TTE-P01, with a bore and stroke of 82 x 47.33cm, developing around 600bhp, made its debut in a McLaren MP4 test car at the 1983 Dutch Grand Prix with Niki Lauda at the wheel. This in itself incensed John Barnard, who wanted to wait for the start of 1984 when a brand

new bespoke chassis would be ready to give the new car/engine combination its first race.

Lauda told Ron Dennis that he thought this was ridiculous, that such a perfectionist strategy would cost valuable development time, but Ron simply couldn't get JB to budge on the subject. Never one to be thwarted, Niki went straight to the Marlboro top dogs at the Philip Morris organisation and told them what was happening.

'They came down hard on McLaren and told them that if they wanted their money, they'd better get on and start using the turbo engine,' recalled Niki with a chuckle. 'Ron fully understood, because I told him what I was going to do. But Barnard was furious. They hated me for that!'

The new McLaren-TAG prototype was clearly very promising and Lauda

rounded off the year with a very strong performance in the final race, the South African Grand Prix at Kyalami. He was running in second place behind Riccardo Patrese's winning Brabham-BMW when the electrics failed. Critics thought McLaren had been grand-standing on light tanks and had run out of fuel in an attempt to impress their sponsors. Nothing could have been further from the truth. Dennis and Barnard kept their thoughts to themselves, knowing just how good their new package really was.

So it proved. In 1984, in the definitive new McLaren-TAG MP4/2s, immaculately prepared by the Woking factory and running on their superb

World Champion for a third time: Niki Lauda on the rostrum at Estoril after finishing second to Alain Prost in the 1984 Portuguese GP. (Formula One Pictures)

Michelin radial tyres, Niki Lauda and Alain Prost carved up the World Championship between them.

It was a season that unfolded into a rare, high-quality psychological battle between the two McLaren drivers. Prost set the ball rolling by winning the Brazilian GP at Rio, where Niki retired with an electrical fault. But the Austrian bounced back to win the South African race at Kyalami where Prost had to switch to the spare car just before the start and was forced to join in from the pit lane after the field had departed. But that didn't prevent him from storming through to finish second behind Lauda. This was developing into quite a partnership.

A calamitous succession of engine detonation problems prevented either car from finishing the Belgian GP at Zolder, but from then on the season got into top gear. Prost won the San Marino Grand Prix, Lauda the French.

John Barnard found that having two such high-calibre drivers was a fascinating engineering exercise. 'Niki was certainly a good development driver,' he said, 'but sometimes he definitely wasn't as good as Alain. The problem could be that he was such a strong-minded person. If you clicked with him in the same direction, he could be an immovable force. But sometimes I felt he was too quick to reach a conclusion, whereas Alain took longer, to be absolutely sure.'

Prost's only controversial victory of the star-studded 1984 season came at Monaco where the race was flagged to a halt at half distance when a torrential downpour virtually flooded the track surface. When the chequered flag was

This shot of Lauda in the 1985 McLaren-TAG MP4/2B emphasises just how little in the way of lateral driver protection was available even less than 20 years ago. (Formula One Pictures)

waved Ayrton Senna's Toleman was literally feet behind Prost's McLaren and gobbling up his advantage.

Ironically, as the mathematics subsequently worked out, Prost would have been better served finishing second to Senna in a full-length race – thereby earning 6 championship points – than garnering the $4^1/2$ that were his rewards for his half-distance victory!

And so the season went on. Lauda won his third British Grand Prix victory at Brands Hatch, then Prost won the German race at Hockenheim. Then Niki won on home soil in Austria after Prost, driving with only one hand on the wheel as he wrestled with a troublesome gearbox, spun into retirement on oil.

Yet this was one of the most remarkable wins of Lauda's entire career. 'I was hard on the throttle in fourth when there was an enormous bang as the gear broke,' he explained. 'I thought that was the end of that, and I began to slow, looking for somewhere to park. Then I began to fish around to see if there were any other gears working. I got third, then I found fifth ... so I thought, "Let's go on and see how far we get."'

With considerable mechanical sensitivity, Niki nursed the car those last ten laps or so to the chequered flag. Nelson Piquet had made up 7 seconds during the lap on which Niki first encountered trouble, but the second-place Brabham-BMW driver couldn't guess at the problem. Thinking that Lauda was just easing off, Piquet failed to counter-attack. Had he done so, the race win might have been his for the picking.

Finally, after sharing the next three

races between them, the last round of the World Championship arrived. Prost and Lauda went into the inaugural Portuguese Grand Prix at Estoril separated by just 3.5 points. Lauda had the advantage, but if Prost won the race the Austrian would have to finish second. Prior to the start it looked as though Prost was a shoe-in for the title. The Frenchman had qualified second on the front row, Niki 11th after his engine lost power as he battled for grid positions.

The tension continued to build on race morning. Lauda was quickest in the warm-up, but his newly installed TAG turbo developed a water leak.

Another engine was installed for the race. Then it was time for action.

Piquet spun on the first lap, leaving Prost third behind Keke Rosberg's Williams-Honda and Nigel Mansell's Lotus. Picking his moments, Alain neatly worked his way through on to Keke's tail. Going into lap 9 he surged through into the lead. It seemed as though nothing would stand between Alain and his bid to become the first ever French World Champion.

Except that Niki pulled off the near-impossible, threading his way through to second place at the chequered flag. He'd had some lucky breaks in the traf-

Alain Prost heads his McLaren-TAG towards victory in the 1985 Monaco Grand Prix where he had a great tussle with Michele Alboreto's Ferrari. (Formula One Pictures)

fic, but on the other hand he'd been handicapped by a broken turbo boost control on one bank of the TAG turbo V6 and was hampered in his effort to get extra power for overtaking.

So Lauda took his third World Championship by the smallest ever margin, half a point. Prost was choking back tears on the rostrum. 'Forget it,' said Niki consolingly. 'Next year the Championship is yours.'

It was indeed. More ominously for Lauda, Ron Dennis had long since made it clear that he wasn't going to pay top dollar for the Austrian's services in 1985 – particularly after he'd got wind of the fact that Lauda had been in abortive negotiations with Renault.

Ron offered him $2 million for 1985.

Lauda told him he was crazy. In the end Niki said he managed to squeeze $3.8 million out of McLaren. But he conceded that Ron had been right 'because there were cheaper guys around, even if I privately believed that I was really worth $5 million as reigning World Champion.'

So Lauda remained on the McLaren team strength for one final season. But in 1985 Prost seemed to raise his game and, in qualifying at least, Niki became a touch more cautious. Alain won in Rio, then found himself disqualified from the San Marino GP at Imola after his McLaren MP4/2B tipped the scales just 2kg below the minimum weight limit.

Alain had spent much of that race

locked in combat with Ayrton Senna's Lotus-Renault and made a mental note about what he regarded as the Brazilian's obstructive driving style. Senna ground to a stop, apparently out of fuel, with two laps to go, but Prost at least made it to the flag. 'I was proud of the job I did there,' he said, 'even though I was disqualified.'

Prost won at Monaco after a great battle with Michele Alboreto's formidable Ferrari, after which came an unscheduled gap on the calendar when the Belgian Grand Prix at Spa-Francorchamps was called off on the eve of the race after the newly laid track surface virtually disintegrated.

In general terms Prost had no problems getting the upper hand over Lauda in 1985, the exception being the Dutch Grand Prix at Zandvoort where Niki slipped ahead when the Frenchman was delayed at a tyre stop by a sticking wheel nut. Niki had started the race – and indeed many races that season – with the avowed intention of surviving his final season. But this one was different.

'I had decided that I would quit at the end of 1985, so all I was interested in was staying alive,' he recalled. So much so that when his friend Herbert Volker came up to his McLaren on the grid at Zandvoort and said, "You're gonna win this race", he responded by asking whether he was nuts. 'I hope my engine blows after one lap,' he replied. Volker looked aghast.

McLaren team-mates for 1986: Prost with former Williams driver and 1982 World Champion Keke Rosberg. (Formula One Pictures)

Familiar story: Prost won another Monaco Grand Prix in 1986, this time beating Rosberg into second place. (Formula One Pictures)

Ready to go: Mechanics make final adjustments to Prost's McLaren MP4/2C prior to the 1986 Canadian Grand Prix. (Formula One Pictures)

'So we started,' explained Lauda many years later. 'At the end of the first lap I was fifth. Then I said, "Right, I'm going to race for Herbert" because the guy was so demotivated after what I told him. So I gave it the big stick, pulled a few stunts and kept him behind to the chequered flag.'

It was Lauda's final Grand Prix victory. He would retire, happily and contented, after the final race of the season. By that time Prost had realised his great ambition and clinched the World Championship for himself.

Niki led his final race in Adelaide only for a grabbing brake to send him into the wall. Yet he'd achieved what he'd set out to do and survived a Grand Prix career that had first started in the summer of 1971. Now it was time for a fresh face to take over his seat in the McLaren-TAG squad.

The man Ron Dennis selected for the exacting task of following Lauda was Keke Rosberg, the charismatic and delightfully self-assured Finn who had won the 1982 World Championship at the wheel of a Williams. When his team stood poised to sign Nigel Mansell as the second driver at the start of 1985, Rosberg told Frank Williams that if he did so he would be off to find a drive elsewhere. He did – so he did!

Alain Prost later admitted that he'd not met anybody quite like Rosberg. 'I was certainly taken aback by his confidence at the first test we did together at Rio,' he said. 'Keke wasn't just any old driver arriving at McLaren grateful for the opportunity. He brushed aside John Barnard's advice to take things easy for

Rosberg prepares for action at the 1986 Portuguese Grand Prix, nearing the end of his final season in F1. (Formula One Pictures)

the first few laps, put his foot down hard and flew off the road midway round his second flying lap. The car was very badly damaged and I don't think Keke and John ever saw eye to eye again.

'Keke was very skilful, motivated and hungry. Perhaps he didn't quite have the necessary finesse to get the best out of the sort of turbo, fuel-consumption racing we had at the time, but he was certainly a great competitor. And a great friend.'

During the mid-1980s the FIA gradually moved to cap race performance from the 1.5-litre turbocharged F1 cars with progressive limitations on boost pressure and fuel capacity. After a brief flirtation with refuelling during 1982/83, this dangerous practice was banned for the start of the 1984 season and a 220-litre fuel capacity limit imposed.

For 1985 it was originally agreed that the capacity limit be reduced to 195 litres, but the teams then had a change of heart and decided to retain the 220-litre level for that year. Ken Tyrrell, whose team was still relying on naturally aspirated Cosworth V8s and sought to block this amendment and insist that the switch to 195 litres was implemented, found himself excluded from the 1984 Championship for a rule infringement. This conveniently meant that he was ineligible to vote and the 220-litre limit remained in place.

Boost pressure limitations remained unchecked for qualifying, but obviously had to be reined in for the races so that the cars would not consume

Ron Dennis with engineer Steve Nichols on the pit wall at Detroit, 1986. (Formula One Pictures)

United by passion for Formula 1

Mansour Ojjeh must rank among the least likely multi-millionaires one is ever likely to meet, certainly in the highly opinionated world of the Formula 1 pit lane. He is a very private, sophisticated and courteous man who never seems to push himself forward into the centre of media attention, preferring to adopt a low-key manner in his role of President of TAG, the billion-dollar company that is a partner of and majority shareholder in McLaren International.

Ojjeh's late father Akram established Techniques d'Avant-Garde in 1975. It originally prospered as a company with trading links with Saudi Arabia and acquired control of the financially ailing Swiss Heuer watch company in 1985, transforming its financial fortunes quite dramatically.

TAG started in Formula 1 sponsorship with Williams in 1979, joining a consortium of Saudi Arabian companies as joint backers of the team. 'I knew the companies, I knew the people,' said Mansour Ojjeh. 'They came to me and said, "Mansour, we have a hole in the budget, why don't you help us out?" I talked to my father and, because of who was behind the Saudi companies already sponsoring Frank, he said OK. Then, in 1982, I met Ron Dennis and we decided that, if we were going to spend money, we might as well own something. So we put together a deal to develop McLaren's Porsche-built Grand Prix engine – and it won 25 Grands Prix and three consecutive world titles.

'We were keen to do something with our investment and there was a scheme to use the F1 engine in a small, high-performance helicopter. But in the end the costs involved were too high for its market.'

TAG's involvement with McLaren was expanded in 1984 when its stake was raised to 60 per cent. 'I take a passionate interest in the fortunes of the team and obviously get a high from the wins,' he said.

It is this passion for Grand Prix motor racing that unites Mansour Ojjeh and Ron Dennis and has been responsible for their deep friendship. And like Dennis, Mansour Ojjeh is a family man who leads a quiet and self-effacing lifestyle with his wife and four children in Geneva.

Yet his unobtrusive personal support of McLaren efforts is appreciated every bit as much as the financial firepower and commercial security that his family business has provided.

TAG's Mansour Ojjeh immersed in concentration. (Formula One Pictures)

For the 1987 season McLaren chose the popular Swede Stefan Johansson to partner Prost. (Formula One Pictures)

their precious fuel loads before the chequered flag. For 1986 the 195-litre limit was finally implemented, and Rosberg found it all pretty frustrating.

'I took part in 16 races for McLaren and scored five finishes,' said Rosberg. 'Call that a good experience? It was the worst time of F1, particularly for Alain and I, because we used to run out of fuel. It was something I could not accept and understand that F1 cars could not, were *not allowed* to carry enough fuel to go flat out.

'In addition, at Williams I had been the leading driver, but at McLaren Alain had been there for ages. And I think I have to admit that I was like an old gramophone record that got stuck in the same groove saying "the car understeers, understeers, understeers." I suppose after six months of this, nobody bothered to listen.

'But it *did* understeer. The best thing I remember was that I went to Alain once, when I was getting really mad about this, because there were one or two occasions when it didn't and then I was very, very quick.

'The TAG turbo engine didn't have the top-end power of the Honda, but the real problem was that understeer. I found it so bad that I was only really able to harness about 70 per cent of my potential.'

Prost failed to score at the first race

The 1987 McLaren MP4/3 being prepared for the 1987 Monaco Grand Prix. (Formula One Pictures)

of 1986, the Frenchman not getting his Championship defence off the ground until the second race of the series when he finished third in the Spanish Grand Prix at Jerez – a race that saw Ayrton Senna's Lotus and Nigel Mansell's Williams stage the closest finish recorded in F1 history for first and second places.

Prost then won again at Imola before heading Rosberg home for a McLaren-TAG 1–2 at Monaco, a race that convinced Keke that he was paired with a star driver of breathtaking ability. After that, the McLarens would not win again until Prost won the Austrian Grand Prix in August, even though his Championshp challenge was still alive at that point thanks to

the fact that Williams team-mates Mansell and Nelson Piquet had spent most of the year taking points off each other.

Prost had an unfortunate skirmish with the stewards at Monza, where he was forced to switch into the spare McLaren-TAG and start from the pit lane. Officialdom eventually decided that he had made the switch 5 seconds too late, after the pack had been despatched on its parade lap. He was black-flagged and disqualified, nullifying a terrific chase through the field from last to sixth place in just 18 laps. It was no consolation that the Frenchman's TAG turbo expired just before he was about to return to the pit lane. Alain let rip to the press as to just

McLaren pit stops were always crisp and efficient. Here Johansson receives fresh tyres during the 1987 Italian GP at Monza. (Formula One Pictures)

what he thought of the governing body and was rewarded with a $6,000 dollar fine for his views.

The Williams-Hondas may have been quicker technical packages during 1986, but there was no way in which the wily Prost could ever be discounted. He finished sixth at Spa-Francorchamps after another terrific chase through the field following a first-lap accident that left his McLaren's chassis twisted like a banana, then took second places in both Portugal and Mexico, in the latter racing coaxing his car to the flag with only a single pit stop for fresh tyres.

In the final race of the season, the Australian Grand Prix at Adelaide, it seemed as though the outcome of the Championship would be resolved in a straight fight between Williams-Honda team-mates Mansell and Nelson Piquet. Yet it was Rosberg, his McLaren-TAG now magically devoid of its customary understeer, who stormed into an immediate lead and looked set to win commandingly.

'I only had to snap my fingers to pull out an advantage,' he later reflected. 'I remember wondering to myself, "Well, if it's this easy, why the hell am I retiring?"'

On lap 32 Prost clipped Gerhard Berger's Benetton as he lapped the Austrian driver's car and the McLaren darted into the pits to change a punctured tyre, dropping from fourth to seventh. Meanwhile Rosberg's bid for a final race win ended after he pulled off at the side of the circuit, acutely worried by a rear-end vibration. Keke suspected that it was an engine problem; in fact, it turned out to be

wayward chunks of a failing rear tyre thumping against the rear bodywork.

Rosberg's retirement alerted the rest of the field to a possible tyre problem, although the discarded first set from Prost's McLaren showed no signs of any abnormal deterioration. But before a

By the '87 season the McLaren-TAG package was showing its age, a fact about which Prost duly ponders. (Formula One Pictures)

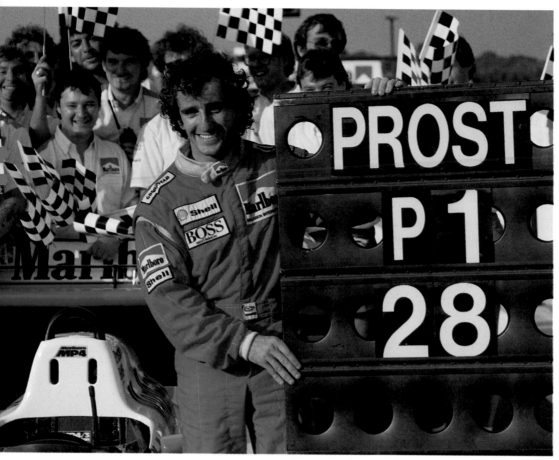

Prost celebrates his 28th Grand Prix win after the 1987 Portuguese Grand Prix. It beat Jackie Stewart's record of 27 wins that had lasted since 1973. (Formula One Pictures)

decisive conclusion could be reached, Mansell's Williams – running second to Piquet and seemingly with the Championship in the bag – suffered a major rear tyre failure at almost 200mph on the long back straight. Nigel displayed enormous skill bringing the car to a standstill without any further damage, but that was the end of his title bid.

Piquet, now set to take the season's spoils, was called in for a precautionary tyre change. Ironically, nothing was found to be wrong, but by the time he resumed, Prost's McLaren was back in the lead. The Brazilian was frustrated in the extreme by this reversal of fortune, yet he could hardly have known that Prost was facing a huge crisis of his own.

The fuel consumption read-out on the McLaren's dashboard indicated that he was out of fuel three laps before the chequered flag. Yet his car kept on running. Just as his tank had run dry in the German Grand Prix when the computer told him there was fuel to spare, now the situation was reversed and Alain duly took the chequered flag to become the first driver to retain his crown in consecutive years since Jack Brabham in 1960.

It had been a great achievement for the Prost/McLaren combo, which had now developed into a classic partnership based on mutual trust, respect and professional admiration. Yet it was beginning to become clear that the TAG turbo was getting a bit breathless as the turbo battle intensified. With three World Championships under its belt, the magnificent McLaren-funded, Porsche-made V6 was nearing the end of its life and Ron Dennis began working on a strategy to gain manufacturer support for his next engine deal.

For the 1987 season there were more changes to the technical regulations, and while McLaren continued to rely on the TAG Turbo it was clear that this would be just for one more season. The 195-litre fuel capacity maximum was retained, but power was further restricted by the introduction of a 4-bar boost pressure limit effected by the installation of an FIA-supplied 'pop-off' valve that was designed to vent the system when the prescribed level of four times ambient barometric pressure was reached.

With John Barnard leaving, Steve Nichols took over as design project leader and produced the McLaren MP4/3, which was essentially an evolution of what had gone before. Visually the new car was distinguished by a lower monocoque and rear deck, the direct result of the smaller bespoke fuel cell, replacing the old 220-litre outer monocoque moulding that had been retained on the previous MP4/2C.

For the 1987 season Prost was partnered by the amiable Swedish driver Stefan Johansson, a move that was regarded by many observers as a temporary expedient. The McLaren-TAGs were again quite competitive, but certainly not World Championship material, and Prost won just three races, including a 1–2 success ahead of Johansson in the Belgian GP at Spa-Francorchamps.

His third win of the year at Estoril proved to be an historic milestone. It was his 28th career victory, beating Jackie Stewart's record of 27 wins that had lasted since 1973. 'Alain produced a faultless performance to win that race,' said the Scot. 'I think he is absolutely in a class of his own among today's Grand Prix drivers. I honestly cannot think of anybody I would have preferred to take my record.'

Yet if Prost reckoned that he had established a bullet-proof family relationship with the McLaren team, things were soon to change. Ever since 1983 Ron Dennis had been keeping an eye on the progress of a young Brazilian who had burst on to the British Formula 3 scene. This, of course, was the astoundingly talented Ayrton Senna, and Dennis offered to fund his F3 career in exchange for an option on his future services.

Senna politely rebuffed the McLaren chief, giving Dennis a taste of just what an independent young man he was. 'I wanted a situation where I simply had an option on whether or not to use his services,' said Ron, 'but what I underestimated was how strong a position he was actually in to come up with his own F3 budget.'

Chapter 5

The
Honda years

Ayrton Senna had been driving a Lotus-Honda throughout 1987, and the Japanese car-maker had become increasingly concerned about its relationship with Williams. Failing to understand the niceties of delegated management, it could not comprehend how Williams could be properly run while Frank Williams spent most of 1986 recover-

Nigel Mansell chats at Alain Prost during an early season Estoril test in 1988. Mansell and Williams lost their supply of Honda turbo engines to McLaren under controversial circumstances at the end of the previous season. (Formula One Pictures)

ing from a road accident that left him a wheelchair-bound quadriplegic.

In Honda management's mind, the failure of either Williams driver to win the 1986 Championship cemented their view. They also desperately wanted to remain involved with Senna, whose talent had been obvious for all to see for some time.

The net result was that Honda switched its engine contract from Williams to McLaren, Lotus very astutely retaining its own deal by the simple expedient of signing Piquet, the man who'd just won the 1987 title with Honda power. McLaren was now poised to sustain its World Championship momentum into a new era.

The 1988 season was the last in which 1.5-litre turbocharged engines were permitted in F1. Moreover, they would be further limited to a 150-litre fuel capacity and a further reduced 2.5-bar boost pressure requirement. It was also a transitional year in which teams were free to introduce the 3.5-litre naturally aspirated engines that would be mandatory from the start of 1989.

'There is no way, gentlemen, for the turbos in 1988,' confidently predicted FIA President Jean-Marie Balestre. But the extrovert French politician had reckoned without Honda.

Honda had a new V10 engine in the pipeline for 1989, but eventually took the decision to fight to the last lap with the turbos. The main engine development priority with the RA168E V6 was reducing fuel consumption to the absolute minimum and boosting power output within the framework of various limitations.

Extensive use of aluminium alloy further reduced the new engine's weight to 146kg, and in order to reduce

Ayrton Senna arrived in the team for 1988. The brilliant Brazilian is seen here at Rio in the McLaren-Honda MP4/4 turbo. (Formula One Pictures)

Engineers cluster round Senna's McLaren MP4/4. In those days the McLarens still had separate, removable upper bodywork. (Formula One Pictures)

fuel consumption the boost pressure, intake air temperature, fuel temperature, mixture strength and other operating conditions were computer controlled together with fuel injection volume and ignition timing. Ceramic turbine blades and ball bearings were adopted for the turbocharger to enhance maximum output and response, while a special fuel was also developed specifically for the engine.

At the start of the 1988 season McLaren kept its opposition guessing until the last possible moment before unveiling the MP4/4. Ten days before

the first race in Rio it was flown to Imola for preliminary testing where both Prost and Senna lapped significantly faster than Nelson Piquet had managed in the Williams-Honda running with unlimited turbo boost pressure back in 1986.

Senna duly rammed home an early advantage at Rio, qualifying on pole position only to suffer gearbox problems on the parade lap. The start was delayed and Ayrton switched to the spare car, starting from the pit lane. For this he was subsequently disqualified, leaving Prost to sail serenely on to an unchallenged maiden victory for the new McLaren-Honda.

The MP4/4 design had been under the guiding hand of the newly appointed McLaren Technical Director, Gordon Murray, the man who had masterminded the Brabham team's World Championship runs in 1981 and 1983. The new cars still retained a generic likeness to the Barnard-inspired concepts that had gone before, but Murray's strong influence could be discerned from the sharply reclined driving position, which Gordon had originally pioneered for the Brabham BT55 in 1986.

From the outset it was clear that the 1988 season would develop into a two-horse race between the McLaren drivers. On the face of it this might have turned into a boring and repetitive season, but that reckoned without

Senna and Prost in practice for the 1988 Monaco Grand Prix. Senna led and crashed, allowing Prost to inherit the win. (Formula One Pictures)

the passionate rivalry that developed between Prost and Senna. Quite simply, Alain was determined to protect his patch while Ayrton was out to usurp the other's position. The resultant confrontation crackled with high-tension static.

Senna won the second round at Imola, beating Prost in a straight fight. He was on course to win at Monaco as well, leading the Frenchman by half a minute, when he just couldn't resist trading fastest laps with Prost. It was unnecessary, and proved his undoing. Senna brushed the wall at Portier, knocking off the McLaren's right front suspension.

'I'd driven almost the perfect race,' he recalled, 'probably the best I'd ever done in terms of qualifying, race performance and car set-up. Earlier, I had a moment in Casino Square when the car jumped out of gear as I began to relax. I nearly hit the barrier. I got myself back into a rhythm, but then the same process happened again and caught me out.'

Prost bounced back to win in Mexico, then Senna was easily on top in Canada. The Brazilian won again through the streets of Detroit, where Ron Dennis received a rough ride from the media when he arrived to explain why he had not let the drivers attend the post-qualifying press conference.

'It is just not realistic to expect us to allow the drivers to be snatched away for more than half an hour at a time when we need their thought-train to be concentrated totally on the technical de-brief,' he said. 'We are trying to make history, you are only reporting it.'

Prost finished second to Senna with the McLaren MP4/4 in the 1988 Canadian GP at Montreal. (Formula One Pictures)

It was a starkly blunt message, delivered with the sledgehammer rather than the scalpel, but the bottom line was that he was probably quite right.

The team returned from North America with Prost leading the World Championship with 45 points to Senna's 33. Alain extended his advantage when he beat the gearbox-troubled Brazilian in the French Grand Prix, but Prost pulled out of the rain-soaked British race, which Senna won at a canter.

Then came more victories for Ayrton in the German, Hungarian and Belgian Grands Prix, after which Prost virtually conceded the World Championship. Senna went to Monza for the Italian Grand Prix with 75 points to Prost's 72. But the momentum was firmly with the Brazilian.

The Italian Grand Prix was, of course, the one race in 1988 that neither of the McLaren drivers managed to win. Prost retired with engine trouble and Ayrton, marginal on fuel consumption and flustered by the fact that Gerhard Berger's Ferrari was closing in fast, tripped over Jean-Louis Schlesser's Williams at the first chicane with only two laps left to run. That left Berger and Michele Alboreto to finish 1–2 for Ferrari on home soil.

Just as it seemed that the advantage had swung decisively in Senna's direction, Prost came bouncing back with a vengeance. Having qualified on pole for the Portuguese Grand Prix at Estoril, Prost squeezed Senna slightly going into the first corner. From the touchlines it seemed nothing more than an uncharacteristically tough

Preparing for action: Senna looks cool and calm as he waits for the off at Detroit. (Formula One Pictures)

Dennis with Prost; their relationship became strained due to the pressures produced by Senna's presence. (Formula One Pictures)

display from the Frenchman. But Senna saw it as a deliberate effort to force him off the road.

The race was red-flagged when some slower cars tangled at the first turn. Senna this time got the jump on Prost, but Alain came swooping alongside the Brazilian at the end of the opening lap. Ayrton tried to squeeze him against the pit wall, but Alain kept coming. After a heart-stopping moment, he was through and away to win easily.

After the race Prost told Senna his fortune in the privacy of the McLaren motorhome – then rubbed in the point by running away with the Spanish Grand Prix at Jerez. Prost now went into the final race of the season with 90 points to Senna's 79, but the Championship scoring system meant that drivers could only count their best 11 results out of 16 races. The bottom line was that if Senna won the Japanese Grand Prix at Suzuka, the title would be his.

It proved to be an nail-biting finale. Senna qualified on pole, but almost handed the title to Prost on a plate when he virtually stalled his McLaren, helped in coaxing it back into life by the fact that the Suzuka start/finish line is on a downward gradient.

Yet even though Senna was 14th into the first corner, Prost could not count on retaining his initial lead. Ayrton was eighth at the end of the opening lap and had scrambled back to second by lap 20. On lap 27 Alain hesitated momentarily as he came up to lap Andrea de Cesaris's Rial going into the first right-hander and, in a split-second, Senna was there alongside the Frenchman, powering through a gap that seemed scarcely any wider than the McLaren MP4/4.

Thereafter Senna remained in absolute charge over the 23 laps that were left to the chequered flag. Such was the ecstatic babble coming across the radio link between the cockpit of McLaren No 12 and the crew on the pit wall that the mechanics and engineers had to remove their headsets to prevent being deafened. It was a well-deserved World Championship success by any standards.

The McLaren-Honda domination throughout that final season of turbocharged 1.5-litre F1 racing represented a magnificent blend of engineering and preparation excellence from McLaren, imaginative technological input from Honda and sheer genius from two of the most talented drivers of their generation. It now remained to be seen whether this level of domination could be sustained through the first season of the 3.5-litre rules in 1989.

The Honda RA109E V10 engine had made its first appearance as long ago as the 1987 Tokyo Motor Show, since when it had been exhaustively developed by test driver Emanuele Pirro. During its preliminary development the new engine had a vee angle of 80 degrees, but after initial vibration problems were experienced it was decided to fit a balancer shaft together with a reduction in the vee angle to 72 degrees.

Relatively late in its development phase there was another significant change when Honda raised with McLaren the possibility of changing the camshaft operation from belt to gear drive. In Honda's opinion this change would offer more accurate valve timing control, but the Japanese company was concerned whether McLaren was prepared to handle the resultant weight handicap and installation problems that this would produce.

Of course, Ron Dennis and his colleagues were anxious to capitalise on anything that offered a performance advantage, even though the change was sufficient to delay the completion of the first McLaren MP4/5s by a

Ayrton Senna in the pits at Suzuka in 1988 on the eve of his first World Championship. (Formula One Pictures)

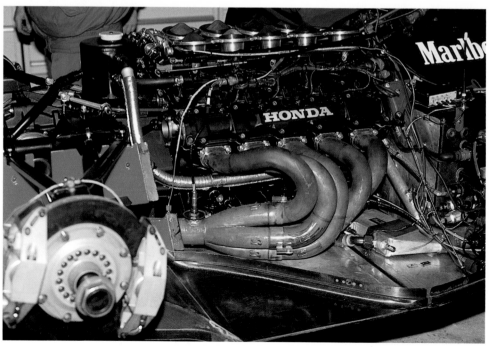

Senna was happy to settle for second in the 1988 Australian Grand Prix, having already clinched the Championship at the previous race. (Formula One Pictures)

Then came the San Marino Grand Prix, the race that caused the tentative armistice between the two McLaren drivers – which had existed ever since Estoril the previous autumn – to crumble once and for all. The two men struck a private deal to enforce a 'no overtaking' pact for the first corner after they'd qualified together on the front row.

Senna got away cleanly from pole position and was pulling away from Prost when the race was red-flagged at the end of lap 4 following a massive accident to Gerhard Berger's Ferrari on the Tamburello left-hander after the pits. At the restart, Prost made the better start, but Senna slipstreamed ahead going into the braking area for Tosa, the uphill left-hander at the far end of the curving start/finish straight.

They finished first and second, Senna ahead. Then all hell broke loose. Prost accused the Brazilian of ratting on the deal, calling him dishonourable. The partnership was spiralling out of control. Soon after the race, Dennis got his two employees together at a test session and made Senna apologise. He did so, but it was only a cosmetic rapprochement.

Prior to the next race at Monaco, Prost told *L'Equipe* what he really thought about Senna. 'I appreciate honesty, and he is not honest,' he concluded.

On track, the battle between the two McLaren-Honda drivers contin-

couple of weeks. The car began the 1989 season using a longitudinal gearbox, although a transverse gearbox was duly introduced mid-season.

The first race of 1989 was on Senna's home patch in Rio, but the Brazilian got tangled up in a first corner collision with Gerhard Berger's Ferrari and Riccardo Patrese's Williams. In the end it was Nigel Mansell who scored a maiden victory for Ferrari ahead of Prost, the Frenchman hampered by an inoperative clutch during the closing stages of the race, which decided him against making a crucial second tyre stop.

Honda's new V10 won the World Championship at its first try in 1989. (Formula One Pictures)

ued unabated. Senna won at Monaco, then again in Mexico. Prost won at Phoenix, neither car finished in Canada, then Alain emerged on top in the French Grand Prix at Paul Ricard, where he announced that he would be leaving the team at the end of the season.

Honda's V10, meanwhile, had not been without its problems. Hemmed in by high buildings at Phoenix, Senna's car had unaccountably succumbed to an electronic problem that scrambled its engine management sensors. Then in the torrential rain at Montreal Senna's engine failed while he was in the lead, the intermittent 'on-off' application of the throttle, which was necessary in such dire conditions, causing the RA109E's oil consumption to sky-rocket due to piston ring flutter.

In practice for the British Grand

The controversial restart at Imola, with Senna overtaking in the braking area for the first corner in breach of a pre-race 'no passing' deal between the two McLaren drivers covering the first lap. Senna and Prost were the class of the field at Imola in 1989, but Prost that felt he'd been double-crossed by the Brazilian driver. (Formula One Pictures)

Prix at Silverstone, where the transverse gearbox was being raced for the first time, both cars fell victim to major oil tank problems. This was eventually traced to incomplete welding within the tanks themselves, and three revised tanks were hurriedly built up in time for the race and the system supplemented by a catch tank through which the oil was circulated by means of a cockpit-actuated valve operated by a button in response to pit signals.

The British race saw Prost win again after Senna spun into a gravel trap due to gearchange problems while leading. Senna came back to win the German Grand Prix, but then had to take second to Nigel Mansell's Ferrari at Budapest. He won brilliantly in the rain at Spa-Francorchamps, then suffered another Honda engine failure – this time due to sub-standard pistons – in the Italian Grand Prix at Monza.

This was the race that Prost not only won, but at which he also decided to announce that he was joining Ferrari for 1990. On the winner's rostrum he chose to celebrate his new deal by

Senna celebrating his win in the 1989 San Marino Grand Prix. (Formula One Pictures)

The eyes have it: Senna had the most penetrating stare, never missing anything going on around him or his car. (Formula One Pictures)

dropping his trophy into the huge crowd swarming around on the track below. Ron Dennis took this gesture as a very public smack in the face for everybody at McLaren. These trophies were not the drivers to throw away and the McLaren chief felt that Alain had been very wrong to do so.

Prost's actions were by now merely the public manifestation of a deteriorating partnership. The Frenchman believed that Honda was showing partiality to Senna in terms of engine supply and the Brazilian driver was heard ranting behind closed doors that his team-mate should be fired three races before the end of the season. 'Otherwise we will be haemorrhaging information to Ferrari,' he argued vociferously.

Prost finished second in the Portuguese Grand Prix, where Senna tangled famously with Mansell's Ferrari, then Ayrton won the Spanish race at Jerez. This left Senna 16 points behind Prost with two races to go. And Ayrton went for broke.

Come the Japanese Grand Prix at Suzuka, Senna qualified on pole by the huge margin of 1.7 seconds, but it was Prost who took an immediate lead after removing the tail flap from his rear wing, a last minute aerodynamic adjustment he made on the starting grid.

Senna studies his lap times at the 1989 Hungarian Grand Prix. (Formula One Pictures)

From the start, Prost definitely had the upper hand. The two McLaren-Hondas hurtled through trouble-free scheduled mid-race tyre stops and Alain retained his advantage. Yet thanks to some superhuman driving, Ayrton gradually hauled himself back on to Prost's tail and – with six laps left to run – made his bid under braking into the tight chicane before the pits.

Shaving the grass with his right-hand wheels, Senna obviously thought Prost would concede, but this was a bridge too far for the Frenchman. Alain turned into the corner and the two McLarens slid to a comical stop in the middle of the circuit.

Prost, who had suspected that Senna might try something extreme, immediately climbed out and walked back to the pits, but Senna signalled to the marshals to help restart his stalled McLaren and immediately resumed the race. In so doing, he accelerated back into the fray *through* the chicane escape road rather than by regaining the circuit.

Despite another pit stop to replace a damaged nose section, Senna drove those remaining few laps like the man on the mission he was. He tore past Alessandro Nannini's Benetton to take the chequered flag first – only to be disqualified from the race for missing the chicane.

The team appealed, but FISA, the sport's governing body, judged that the Suzuka stewards had taken a remarkably lenient attitude to Senna's behaviour. After much extended deliberation, they imposed a $100,000 fine and a six-month suspended ban on the McLaren driver.

Senna was distraught, but nothing could alter the fact that he had lost the 1989 World Championship to his bitter rival. The season ended with an almost defiant performance from the Brazilian who speedboated away from the pack in horrendous conditions of rain and zero visibility in the

Prost was feeling world-weary by the middle of 1989 and soon decided to leave the team. (Formula One Pictures)

Australian Grand Prix at Adelaide. This lasted until lap 14 when he slammed into the back of Martin Brundle's Brabham; Prost, true to his pre-race word, withdrew from the race at the end of the opening lap, deciding that he wasn't going to risk his life in the atrocious conditions.

Meanwhile, the TAG McLaren group was expanding fast. In March 1989 McLaren Cars was established with the objective of designing and manufacturing a unique high-performance road car. This would eventually emerge in 1992 as the remarkable McLaren F1, powered by a 6-litre BMW V12 engine.

This programme was overseen by Gordon Murray, who was therefore lost to the McLaren F1 programme, as was engineer Steve Nichols, who decided to follow Prost to Ferrari. In addition, January 1989 had also seen the formation of TAG Electronic Systems, an offshoot established to provide complete electronic management and control systems in the low-to-medium-range automotive market.

TAG Electronic Systems would soon develop into a highly successful operation with outside customers including Alfa Romeo, Peugeot, Porsche and Toyota. By 1998 the company employed 125 people in a 27,000sq ft production and office complex adjacent to the McLaren F1 headquarters.

On the Formula 1 front, Senna dithered around over whether or not to pay his $100,000 fine to the governing body, only coming up with the cash

Senna in the McLaren-Honda MP4/5 V10 in the 1989 Portuguese Grand Prix. (Formula One Pictures)

TAG plans UK's first business airport

McLaren's links with the aviation world were strengthened in 1998 when Mansour Ojjeh, on behalf of the TAG Group, signed a 99-year lease with the Ministry of Defence to operate Farnborough airport, just 12 miles from the TAG McLaren head-quarters at Woking.

This was all part of a plan by TAG to turn the facility into the UK's first business aviation airport with facilities that would be unmatched across Europe.

'Farnborough is ideally placed to cater for London's business needs,' said Waleed Yousseff, the managing director of TAG Aviation Group UK Ltd. 'The airfield has a long runway, so it's suitable for long haul flights, it is very close to the motorway and only a short drive from London.'

The investment in Farnborough complements the TAG Group's existing aviation interests. TAG Aeronautics is the exclusive representative and distributor in the Middle East for the Canadair jet aircraft manufactured by the Canadian Bombardier company.

In 1997 the TAG Group bought 15 Global Express 19-seater executive jets. These enhanced TAG's ownership of the Geneva-based Aeroleasing company, Europe's largest jet charter operator. In addition, the company's aviation interests have also been expanded by the acquisition of Aviation Methods Incorporated, a San Francisco-based aircraft management and charter company which manages more than 50 planes.

when it really did look as though FISA President Jean-Marie Balestre was prepared to front him down and prevent him from racing in 1990.

Senna would be partnered by the genial Austrian driver Gerhard Berger, who signed a three-year deal to drive for McLaren from the start of the new season.

McLaren's challenge wavered throughout 1990. The uprated V10-engined MP4/5B was competitive enough, but was neither sufficiently reliable nor had adequately consistent handling. With eight races completed Prost had 41 points to Senna's 39 and the Brazilian clearly had his hands full battling his old rival's very impressive Ferrari 641.

By the middle of the season Senna was deeply concerned about the performance drop-off being experienced by McLaren and, as he approached the end of his initial three-year contract with the team, harnessed the situation shamelessly when it came to negotiating a new deal.

Senna wanted $12 million to remain with McLaren in 1991, and, in order to help his cause, cynically wound Honda off the clock by sowing the seeds of doubt in their corporate mind about McLaren's technical capability.

Out on the Championship trail, meanwhile, the points advantage fluttered between Prost and Senna for much of the summer. After the Brazilian took second place to Nigel

Mansell's Ferrari at Estoril, Prost was left trailing. But a week later the Frenchman won the Spanish GP at Jerez and suddenly it was Senna 78 points, Prost 69, with two races left to run.

Then all hell let loose at Suzuka where Senna again qualified on pole only to be told he would be starting from the dirtier, right-hand side of the circuit. He was furious. On the Wednesday prior to the race he had asked the organisers if they would move pole over to the left, on the cleaner racing line. Ironically, Prost agreed with his viewpoint.

The organisers declined his invitation, pointing out that the grid had already been marked out with pole on the right. This handed Prost – who had qualified second – the better line,

while stoking Ayrton up into a great rage. 'If he's ahead of me into the first corner, he'd better not turn it, because he's not going to make it,' he warned.

And, lo, it came to pass. Prost got off the line first and was deliberately rammed off the circuit by Senna at the first corner. No sanction was ever imposed on Senna who, by means of this duplicity, won the 1990 World Championship. The incident left a daunting chasm between the two men that they only began to bridge, rather tentatively, on the eve of Ayrton's fatal accident at Imola three and a half years later.

For the 1991 season Honda produced its third engine configuration in as many seasons with the introduction of the 60-degree RA121E V12. An agreement was concluded to supply

Ron Dennis with the massed ranks of winning McLarens in the reception area of the team's factory in Albert Road, Woking. (Formula One Pictures)

80

the discarded V10s to the Tyrrell team on a 'fixed specification' basis and McLaren began testing the V12 within weeks of the end of the 1990 season.

Much of that development work was carried out by Gerhard Berger in addition to contracted test drivers Jonathan Palmer and Allan McNish. For his part, Senna spent most of the winter resting up in his native Brazil and, on his return to the wheel, made it quite clear to Honda that they had fallen behind on engine development.

Clearly, the new McLaren MP4/6 – with its significantly revised profile reflecting input from ex-Ferrari aerodynamicist Henri Durand – did not have sufficient performance edge to decisively eclipse the emergent Williams-Renault FW14 despite the Honda engine's reputed 720bhp.

Nevertheless, from the outset McLaren played the reliability card to brilliant effect. While the new Williams struggled, Senna won the first four races of the year at Phoenix, Interlagos, Imola and Monaco. At the same time Honda pulled out all the stops to address some of the problems with the new V12, realising that their engine was not only thirstier than originally anticipated but also suffered from excessive internal frictional losses and was prone to main bearing failures, which stemmed from unbalanced oil distribution to the crankshaft.

Meanwhile, over at Williams, Nigel Mansell was getting into his stride. After finishing a distant third in the

Ambition realised: Ayrton on the rostrum having won his home Grand Prix for the first time in 1991. Riccardo Patrese (left) and Senna's team-mate Gerhard Berger were second and third. (Formula One Pictures)

Berger had much to be thoughtful about during his three years at McLaren, which yielded only three Grand Prix wins. He was a loyal team-mate to Senna even though he found himself cast very much in a supporting role. (Formula One Pictures)

Mexican Grand Prix, outgunned comprehensively by both Mansell (second) and Riccardo Patrese (first), Ayrton began to realise that the torch was poised to pass from McLaren to Williams. 'Unless we change our equipment pretty fast, we're going to have trouble later this season,' he said firmly.

Mansell then went on to win the French, British and German Grands Prix, the latter two events seeing Senna hampered by an inaccurate fuel computer, which had his tanks running dry on the last lap of each event.

These problems put a dramatic perspective on the difficulties involved in accurately monitoring the fuel consumption rate of the Honda V12 engine at a time when Shell was experimenting with different fuel specifications. However, thanks to collaboration with TAG Electronics this challenging issue was eventually resolved and Honda really cracked on with development to produce a revised V12 capable of running to almost 15,000rpm for Senna's exclusive use at the Hungarian Grand Prix.

Senna qualified on pole at Budapest and led every lap to put McLaren back in the winners' circle. He followed that

Happy man – not that Senna had a great deal to smile about in 1992, the year he lost the Championship to Nigel Mansell. (Formula One Pictures)

up with another success in Belgium, but Mansell's Williams beat him at Monza. Thankfully, Ayrton had done enough in those early races of the season to guarantee himself an adequate points' cushion as the 1991 programme moved towards its conclusion.

In the Portuguese Grand Prix at Estoril Senna had to be content with second place behind Patrese, then a frustrated fifth – after a spin – in the inaugural Spanish Grand Prix held at Barcelona's new Circuit de Catalunya. Finally, Senna was able to secure his third World Championship in the Japanese Grand Prix – the penultimate race of the year – where Mansell spun off while running third in the early stages.

That slip from the Englishman meant that the title was now Senna's, whatever the outcome of the race, and he had no hesitation in obeying team orders to hand the race win to team-mate Gerhard Berger in the closing moments of the session. This could have been executed with a little more generosity – rather than standing on the brakes only yards from the line, Ayrton could have allowed Berger to overtake more subtly – but it was a just

Ron Dennis plugs in for a word with Senna at the 1992 Spanish GP. (Formula One Pictures)

Senna at speed in 1992 with the McLaren MP4/7, a car that brought new standards of monocoque construction to McLaren. (Formula One Pictures)

consolation prize for a good team player who fulfilled a loyal and consistent supporting role.

By this stage Ron Dennis could detect that Honda's commitment to Formula 1 was very definitely on the wane. From the very start of the 1992 season the Williams-Renault FW14B, complete with active suspension, anti-lock brakes and power steering, rewrote the parameters of Grand Prix car design. Honda was now well behind the game.

Not only was Honda lagging technically, but development of the latest 75-degree RA122E/B V12 was well behind schedule. Much of this lateness was down to the extra effort needed to bring the previous year's V12 up to par. The debut of the new McLaren MP4/7A was initially planned for the Spanish Grand Prix – round four of the Championship – then brought forward to the Brazilian race, which was the third round.

Senna would win three of the season's 16 races in the MP4/7A, but the World Championship went to Nigel Mansell and Williams, who steamrollered the opposition to such brilliant effect that he had clinched the title by the Hungarian Grand Prix in mid-August. Honda had also made it clear that its decision to quit Formula 1 at the end of the season was a non-negotiable issue.

Ron Dennis clearly explained his team's strategy in bringing forward the race debut of the MP4/7 by one month. 'The decision to accelerate the programme was as a result of the performance we saw from the Williams FW14B, both in testing immediately prior to the first race and in the South African Grand Prix itself,' he said.

'In that race, we thought we would be able to run a close third and fourth, but were in fact only able to run a

distant third and fifth. As a consequence there seemed no point in delaying the debut of the MP4/7 because the question of mechanical reliability, which I thought might be a factor in the early races, just wasn't a problem with Williams.

'They clearly had a reliable package from the outset, so in order to stand a chance of winning the World Championship we just had to get the new car up and running as soon as possible.'

However, during the course of the patchy 1992 season, Senna had been quite outspoken in his criticism of the McLaren team's overall performance. Dennis took a philosophical attitude to these complaints, rightly feeling that they were a small price to pay if it

Senna sits and spectates after his McLaren-Honda suffered engine failure during practice for the 1992 Japanese GP. (Formula One Pictures)

meant retaining the services of the best driver in the business.

'I think this year Ayrton has been exceptionally good in the car at race meetings,' he said. 'But I don't think he has had the mental commitment to our testing, which has made life no easier and, of course, he has been very distracted out of the car for a range of reasons. But that distraction has not been counter-productive in terms of moving forward.'

That 'range of reasons' referred to by Dennis included Senna showing more than a passing interest in a deal to drive for the Williams team in 1993. With Nigel Mansell's World Championship-winning season blighted by problems negotiating a new deal with his employers, which would eventually see him quit Formula 1 for the US IndyCar scene, Senna tried to exploit that air of uncertainty by offering to drive for Williams for nothing. However, Alain Prost was already committed to leading this team, and after the two men discussed it frankly, they both realised that it was doubtful whether they could make such a revived partnership work.

Chapter 6

Turning it all around

For the 1993 season McLaren faced major problems. There was no obvious works engine deal available to replace the Honda, so Ron Dennis duly secured a supply of Renault V10s by negotiating the purchase of the Ligier team – together with its Renault engine supply contract.

The idea was then to switch the Renault engines to McLaren, then negotiate for another engine supplier to service Ligier. Dennis secured the agreement of Renault that they would run the McLaren engines on Shell fuel and lubricants for one year, then review the situation. But Elf, Renault's long-time fuel partner, vetoed the deal. Dennis would not break his Shell contract, so the McLaren-Renault alliance never got off the starting grid.

In the event, McLaren opted to become a customer for the Ford-

Michael Andretti, the IndyCar star, took over the second McLaren seat from Gerhard Berger in 1993. (Formula One Pictures)

Senna awaiting the start of the 1993 South African Grand Prix, where he would give best to his arch rival Prost. (Formula One Pictures)

Cosworth HB V8 engine, a reputed £6 million investment enhanced by technical input from TAG Electronics. Due to the relatively late decision over engine supply, the new McLaren MP4/8 was late being completed, which meant that the team's new driver, Michael Andretti, had to test with the old McLaren-Honda MP4/7A up to the end of 1992 – then sit twiddling his thumbs for a frustrating six weeks waiting for the new car to be readied.

Senna's first encounter with the McLaren-Ford during testing at Silverstone produced a highly positive impression. However, lack of a works engine contract meant that his commitment was initially presented as a race-by-race deal.

This left Ron Dennis facing the nerve-racking task of attempting to prise extra money out of the existing sponsors in an effort to match Ayrton's financial aspirations, reputedly $1 million per race.

Whatever the deal, it certainly looked like money well spent. Senna finished second to Alain Prost's Williams FW15C in the opening South African Grand Prix at Kyalami, then reeled off a couple of magnificent wet-weather wins at Interlagos and Donington Park.

Come the fourth round of the title chase, Senna's participation looked questionable. Dennis fell out with Benetton – the works Ford contracted

Surely Senna's greatest race

Ayrton Senna produced many brilliant driving feats, but surely none ranks with his mesmeric victory in the 1993 European Grand Prix at Donington Park at the wheel of the Ford HB-engined McLaren MP4/8. It was a splendid way to mark the only occasion in post-war racing history that an F1 World Championship qualifying round has been held at the famous British track near Derby.

Staging the event was a lifetime's ambition for Tom Wheatcroft, the Leicester building magnate who as a lad had watched the legendary Auto Union drivers Bernd Rosemeyer and Tazio Nuvolari win at Donington in 1937 and 1938. He'd bought the track in the late 1960s, re-opened it to motor racing in 1977 and now – finally – staged a Grand Prix. And Ayrton repaid that commitment with a truly epic performance.

Having given best to the more powerful Williams-Renault FW15Cs of Alain Prost and Damon Hill in qualifying, Senna took the rain-soaked race by the throat from the start, slicing through from fifth place going into the first corner to snatch the lead from Prost even before the end of the opening lap.

The track conditions were wet-dry-wet throughout the race and Senna amazed his rivals by setting fastest lap of the race on the 57th tour – when he actually came into the pits for tyres, saw that his crew was not ready for him and accelerated out again. Even though the topography of the pit lane entrance meant that he had travelled a slightly shorter distance than if he'd been on the circuit, it was still a remarkable achievement and the lap was allowed.

'I am speechless, really over the moon,' said Ayrton at the end of an afternoon that had seen him add this magnificent win to his home victory at Interlagos in the previous round of the title chase. Those were sentiments undoubtedly shared by the bedraggled fans. They may have been soaked to the skin, but it had certainly been worth it for the magic they had witnessed.

Ayrton Senna scored possibly the most outstanding win of his career with the McLaren-Ford MP4/8 in the 1993 European GP at Donington Park. (Formula One Pictures)

team – over plans for a joint development programme on the Cosworth HB V8 engine. Benetton would only agree such a deal on a two-year basis, but Dennis wanted to keep his own options open for a possible manufacturer works deal in 1994 and would not sign up for those terms.

This meant that Senna would not benefit from parity of engine specification with Benetton team leader Michael Schumacher until the British Grand Prix, five races later, and there was acute concern that Senna might abandon his title quest until that point. As cynical observers pointed out, this would also have the secondary benefit of devaluing any successes that Prost might achieve.

Senna kept everybody guessing at Imola. He arrived in Rome on Friday morning on the overnight Alitalia flight from Sao Paulo, and a private jet immediately whisked him to Bologna. A helicopter then transported him to the Imola paddock where he arrived 5 minutes before the start of Friday free practice. It was brinkmanship of the highest order. Not that it did him much good – he retired with hydraulics problems after 42 laps.

Senna scored his third win of the season with an all-time record sixth victory at Monaco, and throughout the

Andretti with the McLaren crew at Imola; they tried to help him as much as they could with data, information and technical short-cuts. (Formula One Pictures)

season the McLaren MP4/8 displayed the team's customary high level of mechanical reliability. Moreover, despite the fact that new rules would ban electronic driver aids from the start of 1994, McLaren continued to invest in its highly sophisticated active suspension system right through to the final race of the season. This certainly helped Senna – who had decided to move to Williams for the following season – to round off his McLaren career with epic victories in the Japanese and Australian Grands Prix.

Senna and Suzuka seemed to attract controversy like bees to a honeypot and 1993 was no exception. Having won superbly – and, one must explain, wound up by his chortling friend Gerhard Berger – Ayrton stormed down to the Jordan garage and asked their new signing, Eddie Irvine, what the hell he thought he was doing. The new boy had been cheeky enough actually to re-pass Senna's McLaren when it was lapping him.

'What the fuck do you think you were doing?' asked Senna with characteristic directness.

'I was racing,' replied Irvine.

'You were racing?' continued Senna, eyes agleam. 'Do you know the rule that you're supposed to let the leaders come by when you are a back marker?'

Senna was meticulous in his attention to the cockpit set-up of his McLarens, taking great care that everything was just so. (Formula One Pictures)

Senna on his way to an all-time record sixth Monaco win in 1993, beating Graham Hill's previous record of five victories. (Formula One Pictures)

'If you were going fast enough, it was no problem,' said Irvine.

Eventually Senna lost his patience and took a swipe at Irvine who fell to the floor, clearly much amused.

It had been a pretty good final year for Senna at McLaren, which is more than could be said for Andretti's spell at the wheel of the second MP4/8. He arrived to a great fanfare following a glittering career at IndyCar. But insufficient testing combined with a limitation on the number of laps permitted in practice and the challenge of handling a car equipped with myriad driver aids all conspired to undermine Michael's confidence from the outset.

He also got involved in too many silly collisions, and the pressure from Ron Dennis steadily grew as the season progressed. Eventually he was replaced after the Italian Grand Prix – where he finished third, ironically, to post his best F1 result – and his drive was taken by test driver Mika Hakkinen for the last three races of the year.

Hakkinen was a protégé of Keke Rosberg and a hugely talented young Finn who won the 1990 British Formula 3 championship before spending two years with Lotus. He then found himself facing the choice of racing for Ligier or becoming

Ron Dennis congratulates Senna after his brilliant win for McLaren in the 1993 Japanese Grand Prix. (Formula One Pictures)

Still struggling; Andretti with the McLaren MP4/8 at Spa-Francorchamps where he was again off the pace in the '93 Belgian Grand Prix. (Formula One Pictures)

'That was the moment I realised just how talented a guy we'd got ourselves,' said McLaren team co-ordinator Jo Ramirez. 'Those cars were really tricky to drive, Mika had never tried one before and he took all the regulars apart. I was very impressed with the way he did it.'

After Honda withdrew from F1 at the end of 1992, McLaren had entered a difficult phase as it strove to forge a new partnership with a suitable engine supplier. The 1993 season had been extremely successful for a team using a customer engine, but this was neither McLaren's style nor a reflection of the team's status within the Formula 1 community. A new factory deal had to be found.

Ron Dennis and his colleagues left no stone unturned. By the end of 1993 McLaren had built a test chassis in which to assess the V12 engine that had been produced by the Chrysler-owned Lamborghini Engineering organisation. Senna was extremely impressed with the V12 when he tested it at Silverstone and was keen to race it at both Suzuka and Melbourne at the end of 1993. Ron Dennis balked at the idea. It would break the established technical continuity of the team, and Senna was moving to Williams anyway.

Yet Chrysler came close to pulling off the deal with McLaren. In fact, it got so close that the US car-maker believed it had concluded a contract in

McLaren's test driver. Shrewdly he took the latter option, a move that would eventually carry him to the World Championship.

In his first McLaren outing, at Estoril, Hakkinen outqualified Senna. Prior to that, he'd only had two race outings all season: at Monaco and Hungaroring he had driven a gleaming white TAG-sponsored Porsche Carrera in the Porsche Cup races. He won both, commandingly.

Mika Hakkinen gambled on signing as McLaren test driver in 1993. He was rewarded with promotion to the race team after Michael Andretti returned to the USA. (Formula One Pictures)

Andretti's disappointment

Ron Dennis has made few public pronouncements he genuinely regrets, but his assertion that Michael Andretti could 'win Grands Prix and become the World Champion' must certainly be one of them.

Those words were spoken at the 1992 Italian Grand Prix when it was announced that Michael – one of the most respected IndyCar drivers of his era – would be joining Senna in the McLaren line-up for the following year. Twelve months later, to the weekend, Andretti would drive his final race for the team at the same track.

From the word go, Andretti's brisk approach went badly wrong. He crashed heavily in the first three races of the year and spent much of the remaining time either spinning off or getting involved in silly first-lap accidents.

'The problem was that he just didn't know enough about the people he was racing against,' said Mark Blundell, then driving for Ligier. 'In the British Grand Prix at Silverstone we were all accelerating away towards the first corner. I had one eye on Jean Alesi's Ferrari to my right, when suddenly Michael tried to go round the outside of him as we got to the braking area.

'I was thinking, "No, no, no ... don't do that!" because anybody with any experience knew that Alesi won't be intimidated. Sure enough, Michael pulls level with him on the outside, Jean brakes really late and starts to slide. That left Michael with no choice but to get on the dust on the outside of the corner. That was it. Straight into the sand trap he went.'

Andretti's distinctive silver helmet in the McLaren cockpit; it wasn't a happy relationship. (Formula One Pictures)

Thoughtful: Mika Hakkinen ponders the timing screen at the 1994 Canadian Grand Prix. (Formula One Pictures)

McLaren relied on Peugeot's V10 for a single season in 1994, but quickly ditched it at the end of the year. (Formula One Pictures)

principle. Dennis vigorously denied this, saying simply that he had agreed that – if a deal was finalised – he would commit McLaren to conducting it in 'a lean management style'. Eventually he went with Peugeot. It was the right choice for the moment. If Chrysler wanted a 'lean management style' from McLaren it probably meant that they hadn't the resources to get the job done.

The McLaren-Peugeot alliance developed with some speed. It was officially born at the start of October 1993, when the first of the 72-degree V10 Peugeot engines produced by former Renault engineer Jean-Pierre Boudy's design team was delivered.

On 20 January 1994 the wraps came off the first of the new McLaren-Peugeot MP4/9s at the team's Woking headquarters. The new car was basically an evolution of the splendid MP4/8, although there were some problems in designing the cooling package as the new V10 engine had yet to run as Neil Oatley and his engineering team finalised their concept for the new car.

Peugeot carried out preliminary tests with their five-valves-per-cylinder A4 engine before settling on the four-valves-per-cylinder A6 for most of the season. Unfortunately most of the pre-season testing was carried out in cool conditions, which masked the threshold beyond which the Peugeot V10's potential for overheating went from the difficult to the disastrous.

Ironically, in the wake of Ayrton

Martin Brundle was the team's second driver in 1994. He is seen here chatting to team co-ordinator Jo Ramirez. (Formula One Pictures)

Brundle's McLaren-Peugeot expires in a cloud of smoke at the start of the 1994 British Grand Prix. (Formula One Pictures)

Senna's fatal accident in a Williams at Imola in May 1994, the FIA did McLaren a favour by changing the technical rules prior to the Spanish Grand Prix. The shorter rear diffusers now required resulted in reduced back pressure through the radiators, significantly lowering the engine's operating temperature thereafter.

Nevertheless, the McLaren-Peugeot alliance was beset by engine problems ranging from detached flywheels to crankshaft pressurisation. Hakkinen was joined in the team by British driver Martin Brundle, the high spot of his season being a splendid drive to second place at Monaco.

Yet this was not without dire technical problems. The Peugeot engines started the races with 15 litres of oil, yet by the end of the race Brundle's Peugeot V10 had no water and no oil left. 'How that car got to the end of the race, none of us knows,' said Martin.

Yet despite Hakkinen's bravado at the wheel, there were no race wins destined to come McLaren's way. Ron Dennis kept a smile on the company's corporate face, re-iterating his loyalty to Peugeot on many occasions throughout the year. But that couldn't conceal the fact that 1994 had become the first year since 1980 that McLaren had failed to win at least one Grand Prix.

Just ten months after the unveiling of the McLaren MP4/9, it was announced that McLaren and Peugeot were divorcing by mutual agreement. The French car-maker entered a new alliance with the Jordan team while McLaren announced a new deal for 1995. With Mercedes-Benz.

Chapter 7

Back to the top with Mercedes

ontinuity of engine supply is probably one of the most crucial elements in contemporary F1 success. From the touchlines, the Peugeot alliance never looked totally convincing. In the end the French V10s were off-loaded on to Eddie Jordan's shoulders and Mercedes-Benz, ready to flee from a spectacularly unsuccessful F1 partnership with Peter Sauber, were only too happy to throw in their lot with Dennis's organisation.

Much time was wasted at the start of the 1995 season grappling with an ill-judged and short-term partnership with Nigel Mansell. The veteran racer, a back-to-back F1 and IndyCar Champion, had become re-acquainted with Grand Prix racing in the second half of the 1994 when he drove four guest races for Williams in the wake of Senna's death in the San Marino GP.

Yet the new McLaren MP4/10 just wasn't up to scratch. Mansell wasn't prepared to struggle with an uncompetitive car at this stage in his career and the partnership was quickly dissolved. But not before McLaren had wasted many man hours designing an enlarged monocoque to accommodate the British driver. In terms of squandered resources, it was a bruising experience.

The alliance between McLaren and Mercedes-Benz also illustrated just how long it can take F1 car and engine suppliers to blend into an effective partnership.

Getting the McLaren-Mercedes to work was a long job, and not just for the chassis-maker. Mercedes's engine-maker, Ilmor, has expended massive effort improving the driveability of its V10 concept. Brand new engines were also introduced for both 1996 and 1997, offering enhanced scope for better installation in the chassis. The work never let up.

The Mercedes V10 engines are manufactured by Ilmor Engineering, based at Brixworth, near Northampton, where Swiss-born engineer Mario Illien and his partner Paul Morgan have established one of the most accomplished race engine specialist companies on the international motor racing scene.

Illien and Morgan both worked at Cosworth Engineering, the manufacturer of Ford's F1 engines that is still based on the opposite side of Northampton. In 1983 they decided to go it alone in an audacious move to beat their former employers at their own game.

'When we left Cosworth, we considered carefully which racing category to tackle and concluded that taking on Cosworth's monopoly in US IndyCar racing would make most sense,' recalls Illien. 'So we called Roger Penske.'

Penske, the patrician multi-million-aire force behind the most successful team on the IndyCar scene, listened with interest to the proposal and liked what he heard. Convinced that he could sell the engine to a major car-maker, Penske decided to back Ilmor's plans and took a 50 per cent stake in the company.

Sure enough, Penske's judgement was prescient. By the time Ilmor's first IndyCar (now CART) engine burst into life on the test bed, he had secured General Motors backing for the project and the engine went on to race successfully carrying Chevrolet badging.

Meanwhile, Illien and Morgan were keen to build an F1 engine, and in 1991 produced their first V10 for the Leyton House team. Unfortunately Leyton House was in dire financial

New dawn: At the McLaren-Mercedes driver announcement in 1995 are, from left to right, test driver Jan Magnussen, Ron Dennis, Nigel Mansell, Mercedes motorsport manager Norbert Haug and Mika Hakkinen. (Formula One Pictures)

troubles at the time and could not pay its bills, even though it legally owned the rights to the Ilmor engine.

Illien recalls that by 1991 he was beginning to get a sniff of interest in the F1 engine from Mercedes as speculation increased that the German car company was on the verge of launching an F1 programme with the all-new Swiss Sauber team. By the time Sauber formally approached Ilmor that August

Norbert Haug, architect of the Mercedes switch from Sauber to McLaren. (Formula One Pictures)

to inquire whether Ilmor could provide engines for his team, the company had bought back the rights to its own engine.

'However, Mercedes then decided that they would not go into F1 with Sauber (yet), so before Christmas 1991 we made a deal with Tyrrell and March to do the engines for them in 1992,' said Illien.

'It was a very low-budget affair, but we wanted to stay involved. But then Sauber decided to enter F1 on his own and we got a package together from the start of 1993.'

Simultaneously, things were changing for Ilmor on the IndyCar front. After achieving considerable success, GM decided to withdraw its backing at the end of 1993, after which Mercedes decided to take over their 25 per cent stake in Ilmor, Penske having earlier sold half his shares to the US motor giant.

Mercedes's contemporary F1 involvement began on a low-key note with the Sauber team, starting with the 1993 Italian Grand Prix at which the Ilmor engines simply carried the identification of the Swiss team. In 1994 the decision was made for the engines to carry full Mercedes identification, but it soon became clear that Sauber was unlikely to develop into a fully competitive prospect.

Instead, for 1995, Mercedes established its partnership with McLaren, since which time it has poured over £30 million annually into Ilmor, enabling its British subsidiary to expand both in terms of workforce and technical equipment. Mercedes also supplements these efforts by making

Nigel Mansell's first test runs with the McLaren-Mercedes MP4/10 revealed a car that still needed plenty of development work. Here a crestfallen Mansell discusses the problem with Neil Oatley at Estoril in early 1995. (Formula One Pictures)

test and development facilities available at its Stuttgart headquarters whenever necessary.

Throughout the fledgling years with Mercedes, Ron Dennis always focused unwaveringly on the task of re-establishing McLaren as the dominant force that it used to be in the halcyon days of the TAG turbo and Honda engines. And not only did he want to win in a technically accomplished manner, he also wanted to win in the right way off the track.

In that respect, Ron believed that those who criticised McLaren for its lack of recent success were in fact offering something of an oblique compliment to the team about the way in which it does business.

'I think this criticism stems from an understandable perception of the way

in which we try to win races, and the way that we try to represent the team,' he said. 'I have a belief that everything is important in life and everything is important when you are trying to achieve high levels of success in any business – certainly in Formula 1.

'I believe that at all times you should have the best – or at least try to have the best. This is not simply about money, it is mainly about commitment. We try to inspire it into the very fibre of everyone's approach to their work for the team.'

It is this basic inspiration that in 1999 continues to underpin every aspect of his whole operation. Not only the racing team, but also the new technology centre – Paragon – currently being built in former green belt land near Woking and designed by

Almost a question of blind faith

During the golden era of Senna and Prost, McLaren seemed to be invincible, with the confidence to go with it. But the team has always worked hard to sustain a consistency of focus during the unhappy times in its history as well.

The period from the end of 1993 through to the start of 1997 was turbulent for McLaren. Not a single Grand Prix victory was scored and the team went from Ford customer engines, through a brief partnership with Peugeot and out into a new alliance with Mercedes-Benz before the good times began to roll again.

'This is a highly financed, very public environment and a failure in it is a very painful experience,' said Ron Dennis. 'With one's engine partners, for example, in times of uncompetitiveness one is far more diplomatic than in periods of competitiveness.

'Strangely enough, these relationships get more strained with more success, but this is normally a productive emotion because pushing hard on each other, and in turn on other people, produces far better end results.

'If you are in F1, you strive for perfection and you look everywhere for improvement, not just in the chassis or the engine, but everywhere. There is that common desire to be better. The most difficult aspect, however, is always to arrive at the

renowned architect Sir Norman Foster. It should be ready for occupation in 2001.

'Winning is not just about winning on the circuit, it is also about winning off the circuit,' he explained. 'Consequently, when people pass less-than-favourable remarks about the things that we do, most of the time those remarks broadly reflect the fact that they recognise that we have higher standards than they have achieved.'

One of the keynotes of the McLaren-Mercedes alliance is that from the outset it has been a partnership in the truest sense of the word. Both Ron Dennis and Mercedes Motorsport chief Norbert Haug have worked hard to ensure that there has never been an apportioning of blame between chassis-maker and engine-

maker when things go wrong.

'We suffered together when things went wrong, and we celebrated together when everything went right,' said the McLaren chief. 'There was nothing to be gained by picking holes in each other's contribution, so when we achieved success we did so as a unified operation. Which is the only way it could be.'

McLaren has also been well served by its drivers in the post-Senna era. Mika Hakkinen is more than a McLaren driver; after five years with the team he is part of the McLaren family. And David Coulthard quickly earned a place in the team's affection when he signed up at the start of the 1996 season.

Even so, in 1996 the team seemed as though it was treading water. In comparative terms its cars had not

same opinion about a problem and to be able to agree how big the problem is.'

In 1994, at the height of the McLaren-Peugeot problems, Dennis noted: 'It's so frustrating, because the formula by which you win Grands Prix is constantly changing. Subtly, but constantly.

'What you really need is the ability to second-guess what is going to happen – not at the next Grand Prix, sometimes not even next year, but what is going to happen in the longer term. You need to be constantly gearing up with that in mind, and that is where I think I need to apply my time.'

It goes without saying that Dennis found the 1995 and 1996 seasons extremely frustrating as the McLaren-Mercedes team inched its way towards consistently competitive performance again. Yet his personal philosophy remained unchanged. He would keep concentrating on what his company was doing, ignoring outside criticisms and influences as much as he could.

'It is almost a question of blind faith,' he said in 1994 in connection with the commitment he was asking from his workforce. 'I never say it, but I think there is a high degree of the "trust me" approach. Don't worry, there is pain before the pleasure, but it will come right.'

When Mika Hakkinen clinched the 1998 World Championship, Dennis could have been forgiven for concluding that 'the McLaren way' had been thoroughly vindicated.

made much serious progress. Yet at Melbourne at the start of 1997, Coulthard and Hakkinen rang the bell.

No more talk of handling imbalances, of Coulthard worrying about rear-end grip, or indications of undue pitch sensitivity. The MP4/12 was right straight out of the box, confirming for once the signals that had emerged from pre-season testing. David Coulthard duly won the 1997 Australian Grand Prix, and followed that up with another victory at Monza.

It would take until the final race of 1997 before Hakkinen finally broke his duck – gifted by the Scot on team orders – triumphing in the European Grand Prix at Jerez, which was where Jacques Villeneuve clinched the World Championship after Michael Schumacher's Ferrari attempted to ram his Williams off the track.

The 1998 season promised to be the best yet for the McLaren-Mercedes partnership. The new MP4/13 was the last of the new breed of narrow F1 cars, running on grooved tyres, to be unveiled to its waiting fans.

The new car was powered by the latest Mercedes-Benz F0110G V10 engine, which weighed in at around 5 per cent lighter than its immediate predecessor as well as being more compact and better packaged with a lower centre of gravity. Its 770bhp power output was enhanced and driveability significantly improved.

The car also raced on Bridgestone tyres instead of Goodyears. The McLaren-Mercedes team made this shrewd switch during the winter after it was announced that Goodyear would withdraw from F1 at the end of 1998. Success in this fast-moving business is all about long-term commitment, and they judged that Bridgestone had the edge in this respect.

Technical rule changes tend to come thick and fast in Formula 1, but in 1998 the revisions to the rule book were fundamental and wide-ranging. The ongoing battle between the rule-makers, who are always seeking ways of slowing the cars down for safety reasons, and the designers, who push their ingenuity to the limits in an effort to make up such lost ground, had taken a more serious turn. With grooved tyres and narrower front and rear track, the best estimates were that the new cars would start the season between 3 and 5 seconds per lap slower than their 1997 predecessors.

By making the track narrower, the crucial airflow over the cars was reduced, theoretically taking the edge off their lap speed by reducing their grip. The grooved tyres also generated less grip, putting a premium on a driver's sensitive use of the throttle pedal rather than simply hurling a car into a high-speed corner and allowing a combination of huge aerodynamic downforce and awesome adhesion from slick tyres to do the rest.

'I think it is going to be pretty diffi-cult getting back to the performance levels we saw under the old regula-tions,' said Adrian Newey, McLaren's Technical Director at the start of the year. 'I'm not saying we never will, but if other people have managed it, then they've done bloody well!'

David Coulthard was understand-ably being tipped by many F1 insiders as a favourite for the World Championship. Yet this was something that made the popular 27-year-old Scot

The Brixworth, Northamptonshire, headquarters of Ilmor Engineering, makers of the Mercedes-Benz Formula 1 engine. (Mercedes-Benz/Wilhelm)

confident and cautious in equal measure.

'It's way, way too early to think in terms of the World Championship,' he said. 'I'll be looking hopefully for an improvement over last year, to win more races than the two I did last year.

'There is no rocket science involved here. It's a car, driver and team. If it all gels and you do your job, the results will be there.

'There is always pressure to perform. But I want to perform. When I was at Williams in 1995, a lot of people felt happy when I finished second, but I couldn't feel good about that sort of result because I knew I had not performed at my best.'

Coulthard said that he did not feel in the slightest bit intimidated by any potential opposition. 'I feel very relaxed,' he said. 'We will be competi-tive, we will win races. Whether that will be enough to go for the Championship we won't find out until, I would say, the fourth or fifth race.

'I am very comfortable with the fact that I can beat all comers. The person who is always regarded as being the best, and who I think is definitely more consistent than the rest of us, is Michael [Schumacher], and I have beaten him twice. Once was in a better car, which was the Williams, and the second was at Melbourne last year with the McLaren-Mercedes when I believe we were in fairly equal cars. I made a better race and he wasn't able to wear me down.

'I know that on my day, I can get the job done.'

This unobtrusive optimism was shared by David's team-mate Mika Hakkinen, the dynamically talented

Mario Illien supervises the assembly of a Mercedes F1 engine. (Mercedes-Benz/Wilhelm)

Finn fresh from breaking his Grand Prix duck at Jerez at the end of the previous season.

'It's flattering that there are people out there saying that David and myself are favourites for this year's World Championship,' he said, 'but Michael Schumacher is the best driver out there at the moment. You have to admit that, because you don't win two world titles by accident.

'It is not always a question of talent, it is how you use it. Michael has taken the best advantage out of himself and the car. But the knowledge and experience I have now should make me a more competitive driver than I was last year. We will just have to wait and see how it all unfolds.'

There is no magic wand that produces instant success in the high-pressure F1 environment, only hard work, focus and commitment to engineering detail. In the fourth year of the McLaren-Mercedes partnership, expectations were running higher than ever before. It would have been unwise in the extreme to have bet against it.

Mika began the 1998 World Championship season as he meant to go on. By winning. He started with the Australian Grand Prix – again gifted by Coulthard, thanks to a pre-race agreement between the two drivers that whichever one led at the first corner would remain unchallenged by the other. Hakkinen led. Then although the Finn, nearing the halfway stage, misread a pit signal, ducked in for tyres and lost the lead, his team-mate ulti-

Mark Blundell replaced Nigel Mansell in the McLaren-Mercedes squad after the 1995 Spanish Grand Prix. Here he is seen at Budapest. (Formula One Pictures)

Ron Dennis looking typically impassive. He took plenty of criticism as he steadily steered the McLaren-Mercedes alliance on to a winning route. (Formula One Pictures)

mately let him through to take the chequered flag in a display of sportsmanship rarely witnessed in modern-day F1. Those two wins, albeit somewhat orchestrated, provided Hakkinen with confidence and he never looked back. By the time he took the chequered flag at Suzuka nine months later, he had won exactly half the season's 16 races to become only the second Finnish driver to take the title crown. Hakkinen appreciated that his maiden victory had been far too long acoming; he was beginning to believe that it would never arrive.

'I would fly to all the races last season thinking to myself "We're gonna win this one". But, yes, there were times that I didn't think it would happen. And when I finally did win, I was surprised that perhaps I didn't feel quite so elated as I might have expected. Then I realised this was because, inwardly, I felt that I should have been winning as a matter of course for a long time. So it did not perhaps have quite the impact. It should have been normal.'

Those who watched Hakkinen and Coulthard apparently toying with the

Mystery man: David Coulthard at the 1996 Monaco Grand Prix where he finished second – wearing Michael Schumacher's spare helmet, which he borrowed after his own was troubled with misting problems. (Formula One Pictures)

opposition to score 1–2 grand slams in Australia and Brazil could have been forgiven for thinking that the McLaren-Mercedes squad was destined to enjoy a season no more challenging than a brisk walk in the park. Yet nobody was underestimating the opposition.

After a slow start, Michael Schumacher and the Ferrari team mounted a spectacular counter-attack. At the start of the year the Bridgestone-shod McLaren was overwhelmingly the best package in the business, but when Goodyear's development programme moved into top gear it was clear that the McLaren drivers had a fight on their hands.

Those two wins at the start of the season gave Hakkinen a valuable mathematical cushion that would work in his favour. In the third race at Buenos Aires he was happy to take second to Michael Schumacher on a circuit the Finn did not particularly like.

Then came the San Marino GP where David Coulthard scored his sole win of the 1998 season, a race in which Hakkinen stopped with gearbox failure. A rogue, counterfeit bearing had somehow found its way into the McLaren supply chain. Steps were taken to ensure that it did not happen again.

Unveiling the new West McLaren Mercedes MP4/12 at London's Alexandra Palace at the start of the 1997 season. (Formula One Pictures)

The Spanish and Monaco Grands Prix produced brilliantly decisive wins for Hakkinen. They were significant because of the sheer high-speed precision he displayed. Starting both times from pole position, he vanquished the opposition to come away from the most glamorous race on the calendar with a 22-point lead over Schumacher.

Yet Hakkinen also showed his mettle when events were running against him. Both McLaren-Mercedes retired from the Canadian Grand Prix, Mika with gearbox problems at the start and David with throttle linkage failure when he looked on course to beat Schumacher's Ferrari in a straight fight. This could have been a crucial turning point, for by this time in the season any success that David achieved was increasingly being regarded as forming a safety net for Hakkinen's title hopes. Take points from Michael and you help Mika — even when Mika doesn't finish!

Ferrari's win at Montreal raised the curtain on a run of three Schumacher victories. Mika had to settle for third in the French race at Magny-Cours behind a Ferrari 1–2, but he drove with great skill in a torrential downpour at Silverstone to lead the Ferrari number

Good start! David Coulthard celebrates a first-time victory for the new 'Silver Arrows' in the 1997 Australian Grand Prix. Ron Dennis and second-place Michael Schumacher share the celebration. (Formula One Pictures)

The Mika and David show

They may have very different personalities, but their commitment to their chosen profession reflects single-mindedness and dedication. Mika Hakkinen and David Coulthard have been McLaren-Mercedes team-mates since the start of the 1996 season, crowning careers that saw both men shine in the junior formulae before making the big time.

They are colleagues suffused with a sense of mutual respect rather than close friends. Cordial rather than convivial, they come from widely varying backgrounds. Mika is a typical blond Scandinavian whose whole personality and approach reminds many in the F1 fraternity of the great Swedish driver Ronnie Peterson. For

New look for 1996: David Coulthard (right) joins Mika Hakkinen in the 'red and whites'. (Formula One Pictures)

much of the time he is undemonstrative, but that placid exterior conceals a twinkling sense of humour and an extremely even temperament.

In the spring of 1998 Mika married his fiancée Erja Honkkanen, who has carved out her own successful career as a roving interviewer on Finnish television. The bond between the two goes very deep indeed, for Erja helped coax and encourage her future husband back to health after he'd come within minutes of sustaining brain damage in a 140mph smash during practice for the 1995 Australian Grand Prix in Adelaide.

David, still unmarried at 28, has always had a reputation as a lady's man. The handsome, courteous son of a haulage contractor from Twynholm, near Kirkcudbright on the Scottish borders, has been cast in the role of every mother's ideal son-in-law. Runner-up in the 1991 British F3 championship, David spent three seasons in Formula 3000 before being recruited as Williams's F1 test driver. After Ayrton Senna's death he shared the second car with Nigel Mansell alongside Damon Hill and became a full-time member of the Williams race team in 1995.

For 1996 he switched to McLaren, having discussed terms for a deal some 12 months earlier. Although he won the 1995 Portuguese Grand Prix, by then Williams had decided to replace him with IndyCar champion Jacques Villeneuve. The team felt that David lacked a certain competitive bite, a conclusion strengthened by his failure to beat Schumacher's Benetton in that year's German Grand Prix at Hockenheim.

Ironically, Coulthard became the man to put McLaren back on the top step of the podium with his victory in the 1997 Australian Grand Prix, and he followed that with a win at Monza before Hakkinen even got his F1 score off the deck.

Out of the car it would be difficult to find a more charming personality than Coulthard. Polite and even-tempered, he is also one of the more articulate members of the F1 fraternity. He and his American girlfriend Heidi Wichlinski, an international model, are truly one of Grand Prix racing's golden couples. Yet in 1998 David would find his resilience and dignity put sorely to the test as Hakkinen turned the tables on him in the most dramatic and decisive fashion.

Mika Hakkinen with his wife Erja, whom he married in the spring of 1998 and David Coulthard with his American girlfriend Heidi Wichlinski, a London-based model.
(Formula One Pictures)

Second win for the Scot. Coulthard heads for victory in the 1997 Italian Grand Prix at Monza. (Formula One Pictures)

wings meant that Mika was unable to keep the Ferrari ace back in second place.

After Silverstone, Schumacher had closed to within 2 points of Mika at the head of the championship table, but the Finn redressed the balance with two straight victories in the Austrian and German Grands Prix, Coulthard in second place.

With 16 points in hand, Hakkinen headed into the Hungarian race at Budapest in confident mood. He led from the start only to be slowed when a front anti-roll bar worked loose on his car, forcing him to drop his pace dramatically. From an easy win, he struggled home sixth after a brilliant performance of car conservation. But he could now seriously feel the pressure with Michael closing to 7 points behind.

The Belgian Grand Prix at Spa-Francorchamps effectively put the title chase on hold for one race. Neither Mika nor Michael made it to the finish. Hakkinen spun out on the first corner, his McLaren then rammed by Johnny Herbert's Sauber. For his part, Schumacher became involved in a controversial collision with David Coulthard's McLaren in torrential rain, the impact ripping off the Ferrari's right front wheel. Back in the pits an ugly scene beckoned as Schumacher squared up to Coulthard, but the episode was defused largely thanks to Coulthard's calm, dignified attitude.

The Italian Grand Prix saw an

one at the height of the storm – only to slide off the road when the conditions became absolutely appalling.

Mika was lucky to find his way back on to the circuit after this excursion, and although he had damaged the McLaren's nose wings it seemed that his 30-second lead over Schumacher would be sufficient to sustain his advantage. Unfortunately the safety car was deployed to slow the field as the rain intensified and that entire advantage evaporated. When the restart was given, those damaged nose

Norbert Haug talking to David Coulthard. (Formula One Pictures)

Mika Hakkinen at speed in the McLaren-Mercedes MP4/13 on his way to victory in the 1998 German Grand Prix at Hockenheim. (Formula One Pictures)

emotional Ferrari 1–2, although the McLaren-Mercedes were certainly the faster cars on this occasion. Disappointingly, Coulthard's engine failed as he was leading, while a rare brake problem pitched Hakkinen into a 175mph spin as he was closing on Schumacher in the second half of the race.

In what Ron Dennis later described as 'the most heroic seven laps of the season', Mika recovered to nurse his car home fourth with only the rear brakes working. It was a great display of damage limitation, but it meant that Mika and Michael left Monza sharing the title lead with 80 points apiece. It could go either way.

Hakkinen now proved publicly that he had come of age. At the Luxembourg Grand Prix at Nurburgring he spent the first 14 laps of the race boxed into third place behind Eddie Irvine's Ferrari as Schumacher raced away into the distance. However, once second, Mika drove a simply stupendous race to emerge from his first refuelling stop ahead of Michael's Ferrari.

It was the defining moment of the season as Hakkinen went on to win in front of the Mercedes senior management. He had proved that Schumacher

Struggling with a serious handling imbalance, Mika was off the pace in the 1998 Hungarian Grand Prix. (Formula One Pictures)

could be beaten, against the odds, in a straight fight. Michael's face was a picture of disbelief as they shared the winners' rostrum. He just could not believe he had been outdriven.

That gave Hakkinen the psychological edge. Five nail-biting weeks remained before the final race at Suzuka in Japan. Michael qualified the Ferrari on pole position, then stalled it at the start, a transgression that required him to start from the back of the grid. Mika had finally broken his challenge. Both men had withstood huge pressure, but at the end of the day it was Schumacher who had wobbled first.

Mika rounded off the season with another decisive win. The first to congratulate him at the finish was Schumacher, the Ferrari team leader having retired with a puncture while running third. 'He deserved it,' said Michael. 'He and his team were the best this year. But next season, I hope, it will be a different story.'

For McLaren, this first World Championship since 1992 marked the final step in their long process of restoration. For Mercedes-Benz, it was the realisation of a dream, putting a new generation of silver Grand Prix cars into the limelight for the first time since Juan Manuel Fangio's World Championship success in 1955.

This view was strongly endorsed by Mercedes-Benz board director Jurgen Hubbert. 'I think this success is very important for the Mercedes tradition,' he said. 'Motorsport is something quite special and belongs firmly to our heritage.

Hakkinen, ready to settle the Championship at Suzuka, 1998. (Formula One Pictures)

Ron Dennis (centre) in discussion with Norbert Haug and Mercedes board director Jurgen Hubbert (left). (Formula One Pictures)

'When we resumed F1 racing again in the 1990s the image of the Silver Arrows was still there, even for those people who had never seen them in the 1930s and 1950s. It shows how competitive and innovative the company is, which is very important in these difficult and commercially competitive times. We are all delighted that Mika has achieved this World Championship.'

The man of the moment allowed himself a twinkle of a grin. As he waited with second-and-third-placed Eddie Irvine and David Coulthard to go on to the victory rostrum, Ron Dennis looked at them all pleadingly. 'Please don't shower me with champagne,' he begged. 'It is just *so* cold.'

Hakkinen just winked at his employer. He at least knew the Finnish for 'no chance'. And he completed the job in the best traditions of Formula 1.

Chapter 8

Design technology is the key

McLaren has never stinted on its engineering and design technology. Each year more time and more care than before are spent on engineering the cars. Attention to detail is the hallmark of McLaren-Mercedes engineering; no aspect of the car's design is too trivial or minor to be overlooked.

The 1999 McLaren-Mercedes MP4/14 is a case in point. The new car, on which Hakkinen and the team's hopes of retaining their World Championship crowns were founded, may have looked similar to that which went before. But it was new, virtually from the wheels up.

To start with, it was powered by the latest 72-degree Mercedes-Benz F0110H V10 engine developed by Mercedes partners Ilmor Engineering. A completely new design based on the concept and architecture of the 1998 World Championship-winning unit, the latest Mercedes V10 had been refined with new levels of excellence in mind.

'Apart from a few nuts and bolts, it is all new,' said Mario Illien. 'It's a bit smaller, it's a bit lighter and we had the aim to reduce the centre of gravity. We were also looking at fuel consumption and driveability, which was a big issue for 1999. However, our main goal was to improve the overall performance and packaging of the engine.'

Emphasising the relentless and continuing process of technical development at the head of the F1 field, the new engine was run on the dyno for the first time on 4 November 1998, just three days after the final race of the season at Japan's Suzuka circuit.

Yet the process of designing the MP4/14 was not something started on one specific day as a blinding piece of technical inspiration. Like everything in Formula 1, it evolved and took shape as part of a process that involves building on all the knowledge and data that has cascaded down the years.

'One of the things that has changed

dramatically in Formula 1, even since the early 1990s, is the amount of development work that is carried out on a Grand Prix car during the course of the season,' said McLaren Technical Director Adrian Newey, the brilliant aerodynamicist who had previously steered Williams to such spectacular success.

'As late as perhaps 1992, the car you started the season with tended to be the one you finished with from the standpoint of its technical specification. The big gains in performance tended to be made over the winter between seasons, but nowadays that development process continues throughout the year.'

In the case of the McLaren-Mercedes MP4/14, its design concept evolved steadily from knowledge gained from its predecessor in 1998. Keeping in mind the relentless and continuous pace of research and development at McLaren, Adrian makes the point that any new Grand Prix car represents simply a 'snapshot' of technical evolution frozen in time.

The very nature of the Formula 1 design process also means that performance improvements are measured in minute terms. Hemmed in by technical regulations that seem increasingly to limit where the engineers can gain an additional advantage, extra speed comes from chipping away at detail improvements.

Long hours spent on development –

One of the race preparation bays at McLaren's Woking headquarters. (TAG McLaren Marketing Services)

Adrian Newey: the extra ingredient

Adrian Newey may play down his contribution to the McLaren-Mercedes equation, insisting that he is just a member of a closely integrated team, but the mild-mannered Technical Director ranks amongst the most respected of today's F1 engineers.

He switched from Williams to McLaren in 1997 – after nine months sitting at home on 'gardening leave' while he served out the agreed severance period of his existing contract – then moved smoothly into the Woking factory. Reputedly, he is paid an annual salary in excess of £1 million. If so, it could be said that McLaren has forged the bargain of the age.

For somebody who left school at 16, and almost dropped out of university because he didn't feel he could keep up, it was an inspirational achievement. The son of a veterinary surgeon, Adrian started out with vague hopes of becoming a racing driver, yet this was always underpinned by an enthusiasm for technical issues.

'I wanted to gain an engineering-orientated degree and managed to get into Southampton University in 1977,' he recalled, 'which I chose because of its motor racing connections. To be honest, I was pretty lucky getting into Southampton, because this OND was not, by then, really equivalent to A-levels. I had a struggle getting in and, once in, a struggle staying there. The problem with the OND was that the maths content was very weak; I wasn't A-level standard, I was O-level standard.'

After those initial academic set-backs, Adrian's persistence in slogging on at university certainly paid off. He graduated with a first class degree in astronautics and aeronautics, and his subsequent position with the March company at Bicester provided the launch pad for his career. He would gain a reputation for considerable innovation in terms of aerodynamic development.

'I took that particular degree course because I felt that racing cars were closer to aircraft than they were to road cars. Add to that the fact that March, McLaren and Brabham all came along to use the Southampton wind tunnel and my interest in this area was sharpened, if you like.

'As a result, my final-year project was on ground-effect aerodynamics. That proved very useful, because when I was subsequently writing round to every racing team I could find addresses for, I could point to this fact. It was also lucky timing, this was in 1980, as ground-effect technology in F1 was really taking off.'

March boss Robin Herd was something of a mentor to Adrian, and the diversity of the company's business meant that the fledgling engineer learned a great deal in a relatively short time. The company was involved in Formula 2 and sports cars, and even built a special closed-circuit record car, but it was on the high-speed ovals of the US IndyCar championship that Adrian really honed his skills.

This led to the post of Chief Designer with the March (Leyton House) team when it returned to Formula 1 in 1988, a role that he retained through to 1990 when he joined Williams to work alongside Patrick Head.

'I think, ultimately, Patrick and I got on well, but when it came to it, he was my boss,' he reflects. 'The title "Technical Director" as such doesn't interest me. But I wanted more freedom, if you like, more influence and, basically, a fresh challenge. I had been there for seven years.

'At Williams I had a very great degree of engineering autonomy, but no influence in other areas. I have more responsibility here at McLaren, and not just on the technical side. It is nice to be involved in other things like drivers, the new factory and so on.'

Newey is unusual in the sense that he still likes to map out his F1 designs on a drawing-board, working to half-scale. 'I just like to have everything laid out in front of me to a reasonable scale, One of the limitations of a CAD/CAM system, of course, is the size of the screen. It is just one of my personal preferences.'

Did he have any particular formula for creating the right environment for his design work? Did he, by any chance, like to have music playing in the background while he was concentrating on the high-tech intricacies of his design work? 'At the end of my first-year exams at college, I listened to music all the time I was revising – and failed dismally!' he replied with a broad grin. 'I'm afraid that's one thing I struggle with, noise and distraction. I like peace and tranquillity in which to do my thinking.'

Adrian confesses that he would be quite interested in designing a road car at some time in the future, but the helter-skelter intensity of life in F1 means that he is concentrating exclusively on a single ambition. To build the best Grand Prix car in the business for McLaren.

Adrian's typical working day sees him leaving the factory at around 8pm for the 20-minute drive to his new home in nearby Ascot. Current pressures mean that there is little time to indulge his passion for old cars. He has a pre-war Jaguar SS100 and took part in the historic Monte Carlo Rally a few years ago in, of all things, a Wolseley 1500. 'Good fun, but a little bit like banging your head against a brick wall,' he jokes. 'It was nice when it stopped. I'm not sure I would do it again.'

Shortly after joining, Adrian changed the rather intimidating mahogany decor in his personal office for a more relaxing shade of duck-egg blue. McLaren insiders confirm that Ron Dennis briefly lost the power of speech when he saw it for the first time.

Adrian Newey, McLaren Technical Director. (Formula One Pictures)

Working on the installation of a Mercedes V10 at the McLaren factory. (TAG McLaren Marketing Services)

particularly in the wind tunnel – may pay off with a benefit measured in tenths of a second per lap. But such an increment is enough to make the difference between winning and losing.

Finalising the specification of MP4/14 was a particularly challenging task because of the pressure of the 1998

World Championship battle.

'Developing the new car was a juggling act because by and large we were using the same people who were developing MP4/13,' said Adrian.

If a team is not actually battling for the World Championship, the challenge of developing a new car for the following season is inevitably much

The McLaren factory floor is light, spacious and kept meticulously clean. (TAG McLaren Marketing Services)

easier. On the other hand, it was a measure of the strength and depth of the McLaren-Mercedes partnership that the team was able to balance the need for continued development of the MP4/13 over the last few races of 1998 with the need to keep on top of the MP4/14 programme at the same time.

The new MP4/14 was the second-generation McLaren Formula 1 car to be designed under the narrow-track, grooved-tyre regulations introduced at the start of 1998. While the development of MP4/13 continued apace through the 1998 Grand Prix season, data was being gathered for the new car, which had to be set against several key timing milestones.

'We set ourselves a deadline as to when the car will be ready and schedule the official launch round that date,' said Newey. 'It is not the other way round. When our cars are launched they tend to take to the track within a few days of first being shown, or in the case of the MP4/14 at Barcelona, a few hours.

'If you see other teams not running their cars for a couple of weeks after the launch, the chances are that they were not completed cars at the time they were unveiled.'

By the time the design of the gearbox and monocoque was completed, the MP4/14's aerodynamic profile had been evolved in the wind tunnel located in Teddington, a few miles from the McLaren International headquarters at Woking.

This process started with Adrian discussing the concepts with aerodynamicist Henri Durand and his team, who went on to produce 40 per cent scale models of the new car. These were then tested in the wind tunnel throughout the summer of 1998 to establish the final aerodynamic configuration.

In addition, Newey reviewed all the data and information amassed by the Vehicle Dynamics department – formerly research and development – which tests materials and componentry for future F1 use. Its work also includes analysis of data gathered from the cars and the manufacture of hydraulic components and assemblies.

In ideal circumstances the McLaren team would plan to have its monocoque finalised by July for the following year, but inevitably the pressures of motor racing usually mean that they are not completed until a month or so later.

In the case of MP4/14, pressure of work on the 1998 car's development pushed this deadline back quite significantly and it was not until the end of

Shrewd switch to Bridgestone

At the start of the 1998 season McLaren-Mercedes took the bold decision to switch from Goodyear to Bridgestone tyres in what was seen by some as a gamble to secure a short-term performance advantage prior to Goodyear's withdrawal from F1 at the end of the season.

But it was a shrewd decision, buttressed by considerable enthusiasm from Mercedes whose CLKs had won the GT championship in 1997 using the Japanese rubber. McLaren's contract with Goodyear extended beyond the Akron company's scheduled withdrawal at the end of 1998, so as the contract could not now be met, it made sense to change camps.

Ron Dennis had clearly stolen a march on anybody who might themselves have been contemplating a premature switch to Bridgestone. The obvious benefit was prestige status as the tyre maker's number one team, the certainty that its products would be tailored closely to the requirements of the 1998 McLaren, and a year's lead over the other top F1 teams when it came to consolidating personal relationships with the Japanese.

Attention to minute detail is the McLaren-Mercedes hallmark. (TAG McLaren Marketing Services)

September that the monocoque design was finally confirmed, allowing Chief Designer Neil Oatley's Vehicle Design department to enter the picture.

By this stage, the other key departments in the factory were also flat-out. The composite shop, one of the most labour-intensive areas, was fully occupied producing the carbon-fibre composite components for the monocoque, body panels, wings and suspension components.

The machine shop, another major manufacturing area, producing machined metallic components, and the fabrication shop, responsible for hand-crafting many items from brake pedals to suspension uprights and water radiators, were also on red alert.

By the end of October 1998 the plastic resin buck from which the carbon-fibre composite monocoque moulds would be manufactured had been completed, a task that had taken Oatley's department around three weeks to design.

The McLaren team, of course, pioneered the use of carbon fibre composite chassis construction in 1981. Modern carbon fibre is produced by heating and stretching acrylic fibres, first in air and subsequently in argon, a nitrogen-enriched atmosphere. This gives the material the strength and lightness so essential for the chassis of a Grand Prix car.

The fibres are woven into a fabric that is then impregnated with epoxy resin and delivered to McLaren whose technicians cut, trim and weave the fabric over the moulds. The various components are then placed in vacuum bags and put into a huge computer-controlled oven – called an autoclave – where they are heated at 120 degrees for up to four hours. The end result is a component one-fifth the weight of steel but twice as strong.

As a result of this process, the first basic monocoque, minus its internal

A McLaren MP4/13 monocoque receives the final touches. (TAG McLaren Marketing Services)

bulkheads and other accessories, was ready by the first week in December.

By the beginning of January 1999 the first MP4/14 chassis were nearing completion with all their internal componentry being installed. The completion of the bodywork, the spraying of the car in the distinctive West McLaren Mercedes livery, and the meticulous application of all the sponsorship decals is one of the final processes to take place.

As paint shop manager George Langhorn explained, 'The new car is more a work of art than it used to be. A great deal of precision is also necessary to ensure perfect inter-changeability. For example, we send six noses to each race and every one must be capable of matching an individual chassis perfectly.'

While all this work continued apace at Woking, the new Mercedes-Benz F0110F V10 development programme was in full flow with work running on the transient dynamometers at both Ilmor's Brixworth premises and the Daimler-Chrysler HQ in Stuttgart.

However, such is the technical precision and accuracy of the relationship between McLaren and Mercedes – and in order to maximise the period of development for the new engine – it has become well-established practice for Ilmor to deliver to McLaren a detailed, non-working mock-up of its Mercedes engines in advance of the completed working unit.

As is customary, the mock-up Mercedes-Benz F0110H unit incorporated all the oil and hydraulic pipes and couplings – and all other points of interface – that would need to match

Ron Dennis in the trophy room with a recent addition to the winning car line-up. (Formula One Pictures)

up with the MP4/14 chassis. The first race-ready engines could thus be delivered to the McLaren factory a matter of days before the final completion of the first car in early February. Without any doubt that they would fit.

Once the new car was unveiled, the schedule ahead included a couple of intensive weeks of testing before a trio of MP4/14s were loaded up for the long haul to Melbourne and the first race of the season. The team had also tested the 1998 MP4/13 alongside the new car to ensure that it had a fall-back position, although this option was never in the event pursued.

Chapter 9

F1's commercial dimension

Ensuring that its sponsors are in a position to maximise their investment with the team has always been one of the main priorities for McLaren. TAG McLaren Marketing Services was originally established to provide just such a service as well as seeking out new investors who might be suitable partners for the future. No other team in F1 is so organised and well-drilled in this respect.

Central to this crucial interface between investors and the team is the Formula 1 Paddock Club, an exclusive environment in which key guests can be looked after and entertained at the races in sumptuous comfort. And at considerable expense.

The Paddock Club is operated by Allsport Management, a Swiss-based company controlled by entrepreneur Paddy McNally, which offers this high quality service to all the competing teams. But it is typical of McLaren's attention to detail that they refine the concept to their own personal five-star formula.

Take the 1999 Monaco Grand Prix, for example. High above the harbour in the West McLaren Mercedes Paddock Club, amidst potted plants, luxurious carpets and the chink of crystal glasses, the atmosphere is as relaxed and calm as the pit lane is frenetic. And for Caroline Sayers and her colleagues from TAG McLaren Marketing Services, the whole exercise involved in looking after the Paddock Club guests calls for the same high levels of behind-the-scenes co-ordination, efficiency and attention to detail as characterises the efforts being expended on the cars of Mika Hakkinen and David Coulthard.

On the face of it Monaco might seem more straightforward than the other races, but the combination of over-crowding, difficulty of access to the street-circuit area when cars are on the track, and pressure on paddock passes make it a far more nerve-wracking affair than at any permanent circuit where facilities are organised to an established format.

'Every aspect of the weekend is a little more difficult and different from most other races,' Caroline explains. 'We had about 180 guests to entertain during the course of the weekend. That's actually quite a small number for us, as we're talking about 300 per day generally – and as many as 700 per day in Germany!' Even so, this can add up to around 600 meals over two days, including breakfast, lunch and afternoon tea, all of which has to be ordered and produced by Allsport management's catering department to a pre-agreed menu.

It costs about $1,000 a weekend to entertain a guest in the Paddock Club and all bookings are arranged by the team which then passes the charges on to the sponsors concerned. Visitors are taken over six at a time – using 'floating' guest passes not issued to a specific individual – to visit the pits and paddock with a member of the TAG McLaren support team to guide them.

'Our Paddock Club position overlooking the harbour is the best position of all, but if you'd come here on the Wednesday prior to the race you would have seen absolutely nothing ready!'

The format by which the McLaren Paddock Club premises are built up at each race seldom varies, apart from at Monaco. Here the TAG McLaren marketing staff have a little more time on their hands, the Paddock Club facility only being open on Saturday and Sunday.

Three days before a Grand Prix weekend begins, the McLaren Paddock Club facilities are completed. McLaren has a contract with a Belgian company – Connexion – which transports the interior from race to race. 'They build it up completely,' says Caroline, 'but we own everything inside the unit, the panelling, televisions, carpets and all the furniture, apart from the tables which we hire from Allsport.'

McLaren take great pains to ensure that all the guests feel they have enjoyed personal contact with the team. 'The drivers come up to meet them a couple of times during the course of the weekend.

'We have guests who come back time and again over the years. These people enjoy a close relationship with our staff. That contact has such a good effect and has, I'm sure, made a contribution to the team keeping its sponsors even when we haven't been winning races.

They remember us and we remember them, which is what it's all about

---

'They remember us and, more importantly perhaps, we always remember them, which is what it is all about.'

The Paddock Club is an essential back-up tool which works as a commercial adjunct to sponsors' considerable financial involvement in bankrolling the McLaren-Mercedes team's World Championship challenge.

Things have certainly changed since

1966 when Bruce McLaren's fledgeling F1 team was funded by companies within the motorsport or motor industry orbit. By 1968, when McLaren invested around £35,000 to purchase five Ford Cosworth DFV engines, it is likely that his overall budget scarcely approached £100,000 in total. This was a considerable sum at a time when the average bank manager barely earned £3,000 a year, but it is small beer compared with the budgets seen in F1 on the verge of the new millennium.

McLaren team sponsors tend to be loyal and enduring

This is consumption at its most conspicuous. And, with a bizarreness not lost on a sport in which the physical fitness of the drivers is paramount, cigarette barons are still the main providers. At the end of 1996, Ron Dennis split with Marlboro, the Philip Morris cigarette brand which had been McLaren's title sponsor since 1974, and struck out on a new commercial relationship with the German West cigarette brand.

It is a deal reputedly worth £30 million, a major proportion of the £65 million annual operating cost of such a leading edge Formula 1 team. The switch also saw the familiar red and white team livery replaced by a striking silver and dark grey corporate image which, given the Mercedes tradition of silver racing cars, enabled the press to hang the famous 'Silver Arrows' epithet round the new partnership.

Both McLaren and Mercedes remain extremely discreet about any sort of commercial issues, but the Mercedes investment in the team is reputed to run at more than £20 million a year taking into consideration the provision of free engines and additional research and development facilities in Stuttgart.

McLaren pays its drivers well. For the 2000 season it is believed that Mika Hakkinen has negotiated a deal worth close to £9 million, with David Coulthard on around £4 million. This compares with Michael Schumacher's £14 million as Ferrari team leader and Damon Hill's £5 million for driving the Jordan Mugen-Honda in 1999.

In addition to sponsorship, McLaren does well out of the F1 television coverage income. This is divided between the competing teams and Bernie Ecclestone's Formula One Administration which masterminds the TV operation.

As Grand Prix racing's commercial rights holder, he takes 50 per cent of the television income – estimated at around £120 million a year – out of which he has to pay the operational costs, while the teams share 50 per cent free of costs. Top teams like McLaren could make as much as £15 million a year from this lucrative profit centre.

McLaren team sponsors tend to be loyal and enduring. They not only get prime exposure on global television – F1 is now the world's third most visible televised sport after the Olympic Games and the World Cup – but they

Honing the team spirit

After eight years as operations director, Martin Whitmarsh was appointed managing director of McLaren International as Ron Dennis took over as MD of the TAG McLaren Group as a whole.

Whitmarsh joined McLaren in 1989 at a time when the company was expanding to the point that Ron Dennis, a perfectionist for whom delegation doesn't come easily, believed it needed a more wideranging management structure. Formerly a manufacturing director with British Aerospace, Whitmarsh had plenty of exposure to high technology engineering and manufacturing processes. What he was now charged with doing was to make McLaren a more efficient operation, but at the same time sustaining the creative culture and fast response times which are the cornerstone of every competitive Grand Prix team.

'We have a situation where Ron and Mansour want us to succeed,' said Whitmarsh. 'They want us to win races, they want us to win championships and they want us to do it in style. And they want us to do it with the right organisation, the right people, the right ethos, throughout the company.'

Whitmarsh, like Ron Dennis, is a strong believer in the team approach. 'I understand that something which says 28 engineers contributed to a new car isn't what people want,' he grins. 'And yes, there are star designers. But there isn't one person who can design a racing car. It is a team effort and managing that team is important.'

benefit from the culture of excellence which the team has worked hard to establish over many years. To be associated with McLaren in 1999 gives a sponsor as much of an exclusive cachet as the sponsorship itself is valuable to the team.

However, in the longer term, there is a fly in the commercial ointment of every current Grand Prix team. The European Union will ban tobacco sponsorship from 2006 and, while the initial response from some F1 insiders was to threaten the effective relocation of the sport from Europe to the Pacific Rim, this was quickly seen as unrealistic.

Leading Labour MP Peter Hain – himself a keen motor racing fan – put the position into firm context with his remarks early in 1999. 'We want to see Formula 1 weaned off its unhealthy addiction to tobacco, but we recognise that you can't do it overnight. The FIA has put forward a very good case for phasing it out – you couldn't just chop tobacco overnight, it wouldn't work – but I would like to see the drivers taking tobacco off their overalls and helmets as a first step.

'The drivers are the ones who inspire young people and if they were encouraged not to wear branding, it would stop that almost sexy image of tobacco and encourage other non-tobacco sponsors to come into the sport.

'Because the tobacco companies pay well over the odds for their exposure,

MP4-98T: the two-seater fit for a king

Sunday, 30 May 1999 was a majestic date for the McLaren-Mercedes F1 team. Prior to the Spanish Grand Prix at Barcelona's Circuit de Catalunya, a race from which Mika Hakkinen and David Coulthard would produce a 1–2 victory, King Juan Carlos of Spain became the first member of any royal family to travel in the tandem seat of the MP4-98T two-seater Formula 1 car.

The 61-year-old monarch had long been a motor racing enthusiast, even though sailing was his foremost passion to the point where he had been a member of his country's 1972 Olympic sailing team.

Now he was to experience something completely new. With Martin Brundle at the wheel, he was driven for three laps round the circuit. 'Today's experience was the ride of my life,' said the King.

Plans for the MP4-98T had originally been revealed a year earlier on the eve of the 1998 Australian Grand Prix. At a media lunch, the excited chatter of pre-season gossip was stilled as Ron Dennis stood up to make an announcement.

Seconds later, Mika and David took the wraps off a quarter-scale model. We were momentarily reduced to a stunned silence, but then the questions came thick and fast. Who would drive it for the first time? Who would be his passenger? Where do we start queueing for the ride of a lifetime? And, perhaps more to the point, a simple 'why?'

For several years TAG boss Mansour Ojjeh had been trying to coax Ron into building a two-seater Grand Prix car so that outsiders might taste the world of blistering acceleration and daunting lateral G-forces which is the everyday environment for today's F1 driver.

Finally the green light was given to the group's specialist subsidiary, McLaren Cars, to construct this remarkable vehicle. Yet it was to be no hastily modified existing racing car. The design brief was to construct a bespoke machine incorporating the highest standards of constructional safety for both driver and passenger.

McLaren Cars Technical Director Gordon Murray and Chief Designer Barry Lett, who led the programme, took a long look at the Rocket two-seater sports car which Murray designed some time earlier.

It provided some ideas as to how to tackle the 'one-plus-one' F1 cockpit layout.

Separating the driver and passenger is a drop-in driver's seat back module, a structural carbon unit which fits between the two occupants and takes up the seat belt loads for the driver. It is a two-position component; so you can have a small driver in the front and a large person in the back, or nobody in the back and a big chap in the front, a privileged guest driver perhaps.

The module also incorporates the driver's head-rest, a carbon fibre/honeycomb composite structure faced with 75mm of conforfoam padding which fully conforms to the impact absorption requirements laid down by the FIA. This is duplicated on the rear of the head-rest structure to protect the passenger in the event of a severe frontal impact. The passenger's legs go either side of the driver and his or her feet can be braced against a specially positioned bulkhead.

The passenger position is personally tailored in much the same way as on the McLaren F1 road car. There is a basic passenger seat to which bespoke trimming elements are added as appropriate.

It was originally intended that the MP4-98T would be powered by one of the 1997 Mercedes-Benz F0110F V10 engines, but lack of supplies meant a last-minute switch to the 1998 'G' spec engine as used in the MP4/13s which were to take McLaren and Mercedes to the 1998 title. This involved a major re-design quite late in the day since the new V10 was built to be installed lower in the chassis, had a different gearbox attachment and a very different fuel system.

The car has been used to chauffeur a

King Juan Carlos became the most famous celebrity to ride in the new two-seater McLaren MP4-98T. (Formula One Pictures)

wide range of celebrities all over the world, from FIA President Max Mosley to violinist Vanessa Mae and a host of competition winners.

It is also used to raise money for two charities. By auctioning these exclusive rides to newspapers and international television stations, the MP4/98T programme had by the end of 1998 raised over £100,000 which was divided between the Tommy's campaign for research into foetal health and KOBRA, a small project to help abused children in and around the city of Stuttgart where Mercedes-Benz has its headquarters.

McLaren has been a long-time supporter of the Tommy's campaign and the MP4/98T programme is the most recent of several initiatives to raise money.

For its part, the Mercedes motorsport division has been supporting the KOBRA charity for just over a year.

the other possible non-tobacco sponsors cannot get a look-in.'

So McLaren and all its competitors know they will have to come to terms with progressively reducing tobacco sponsorship over the next few years, and fresh alliances must be explored and exploited. Diversification must be the key to long-term survival and prosperity.

It was with that in mind that McLaren stunned the paddock at the 1999 British Grand Prix when Ron Dennis announced that Daimler Chrysler – owners of Mercedes-Benz – had taken an option to purchase a 40 per cent stake in the TAG McLaren Group.

Both parties are bound by on-disclosure agreements in respect of the terms and conditions of the deal, but motor industry observers put the cost of the stake between £80 million and £100 million.

It was the second major coup in as many days for the Anglo German partnership, coming just 24 hours after confirmation that McLaren Cars will build the forthcoming 540bhp AMG V8-engined Mercedes SLR supercar – starting in the year 2002 – at the new TAG McLaren headquarters, Paragon, which is currently under construction near Woking.

'This element of our long-term strategy is designed to further enhance our products and to differentiate the Mercedes-Benz brand in an increasingly competitive market,' said Daimler Chrysler chairman Jurgen Schrempp.

In motor racing terms, the link

The Paddock Club, a crucial interface between investors and the team. (Formula One Pictures)

strengthens immeasurably the McLaren-Mercedes F1 programme which, Ron Dennis was quick to emphasise, remains the McLaren core business.

'It is absolutely essential to our strategy to keep a dominant position in F1,' he said, confirming that under the new arrangement he and TAG boss Mansour Ojjeh would each retain 30 per cent stakes in TAG McLaren.

'The new project will have no impact at all on the F1 budget. We are well structured and disciplined in the handling of our F1 budget. It is certainly not necessary for Daimler Chrysler to provide additional funding for F1.'

Daimler Chrysler board member Dr Jurgen Hubbert made it clear that there were no plans to take more than a minority share in TAG McLaren. 'It is a relationship which is more than just business.'

Dennis confirmed that 'one of the pre-requisites from Mr Schrempp was that there should be nothing in place to detract from the (McLaren) entrepreneurial spirit. That value cannot be stripped out of the company.'

The new SLR will officially be dubbed a Mercedes-Benz McLaren. 'McLaren is a strong brand,' said Dennis, 'and we believe it will bring added value to this particular car.'

Chapter 10

Race weekend

Walk into any Grand Prix paddock in Europe and you will find that the steely silver-grey McLaren and Mercedes transporters and support vehicles stand out like new pins, even among the brilliant high-tech machinery from the other teams.

Around 60 personnel attend each Grand Prix under the direction of Ron Dennis, Norbert Haug, Adrian Newey, Mario Illien, Race Team Manager Dave Ryan and Team Co-ordinator Jo Ramirez.

Each of the team's race cars has three engineers and three mechanics allocated to it, with three additional mechanics looking after the spare car. Below the management strata, the race team personnel who are responsible for the cars driven by Hakkinen and Coulthard are Steve Hallam, the immensely experienced former Lotus technician who is head of race engineering, and the team's chief mechanic Mike Negline.

Supporting the efforts of these key individuals are an array of unsung heroes including two data analysis technicians, eight engine support engineers, seven truck drivers, two Bridgestone tyre engineers, Mobil fuel and lubricant specialist Dr Tony Harlow, and a couple of physiotherapists. In addition there are several members of the TAG McLaren Marketing Services staff, press officers Anna Guerrier from McLaren and Wolfgang Schattling from Mercedes-Benz, the hospitality and catering staff and a host of guests, mostly from companies who are involved with McLaren as team sponsors or suppliers.

The purpose-built transporters are all pulled by Mercedes-Benz towing rigs. The main McLaren transporter brings along the team's three cars for the weekends while a secondary truck brings along a full workshop, including a lathe, milling machine and all the requisite fabricating equipment that may be required to do the job. This truck also has lockers containing the drivers' overalls, a larder and two refrigerators.

Supporting the transporters are three motorhomes, a conventional single-decker affair for Mercedes and a pair of 'collapsible' two-storey structures that are home for McLaren and West, the team's title sponsor.

These specially designed motorhomes have upper decks that rise to a full height of 5 metres at the touch of a hydraulic button. The West motorhome contains an office where the race team can discuss and debrief, while the McLaren version includes Ron Dennis's office, which has satellite communications back to the factory in Britain as well as the ability to lock

into all the team's radio networks at the track concerned.

Once the entire West McLaren Mercedes encampment has established its bridgehead in the paddock earlier in the week, a task that takes an enormous amount of physical and administrative effort from virtually the entire workforce, pressure inexorably starts to ramp up in preparation for the race on Sunday.

On Thursday afternoon there is a team briefing with the drivers to discuss the set-up of their cars and discuss the possible strategies to be used in quite general terms. Much of the data used at these discussions will have been derived from pre-race test sessions, either at that circuit or else-

David Coulthard with Ron Dennis outside the team's latest motorhome. (Formula One Pictures)

where. There will also be discussions with the Bridgestone tyre technicians over the choice of the two available rubber compounds supplied for each race.

Friday sees two hour-long sessions of free practice, from 11.00 to 12.00, and 13.00 to 14.00. Then Hakkinen and Coulthard will go into another debrief with the engineers, as the result of which job lists will be issued to Mike Negline and his colleagues relating to such things as set-up, gear ratios and tyre choice. Each evening the mechanics will all dine under the awning of the West motorhome, enjoying the culinary expertise of Lyndy Woodcock and the staff of Absolute Choice, the catering company that deals exclusively with the team's catering in the paddock.

The mechanics will probably get back to their hotels by 8 or 9 o'clock in the evening, and most prefer as early a night as possible, mindful that Saturday and Sunday both bring with them 5.00am starts. Saturday's free practice session is divided into two 45-minute stints, from 9.00 to 9.45 and 10.15 to 11.00, after which there are just two hours to make any key adjustments to the cars before Mika and David take to the circuit for the hour-long qualifying session, in which they are permitted to complete just 12 laps apiece.

During that break the two drivers may take the opportunity of a massage

The West McLaren Mercedes enclave in the paddock at the 1999 San Marino Grand Prix. On either side are the two unique 'expandable top' motorhomes used by McLaren and West respectively with the single-decker Mercedes motorhome in the centre. (Formula One Pictures)

Irvine considered as Coulthard replacement

As early as the 1999 German Grand Prix both Mika Hakkinen and David Coulthard were signed up again as the McLaren-Mercedes drivers for the 2000 season and beyond. However although retaining Hakkinen was an absolute priority, the team did briefly consider Eddie Irvine as an alternative to the pleasant Scottish driver who first joined the team in 1996.

Ron Dennis would not be drawn on the terms of the deal. 'It would be inappropriate to discuss the terms of the contract, but the consistency represented by this agreement reflects the personal strength and depth of our relationships with both our drivers.'

The 28-year-old Scot said he was 'ecstatic' at having secured a new contract only a week after the most embarrassing moment of his F1 career when he pushed his team-mate off the road on the second corner of the Austrian Grand Prix.

Dennis had previously admitted that the management owed it to the team as a whole to explore every realistic option on the driver front and there were those who rated Irvine – Ferrari's number two driver since 1996, who had come into his own so spectacularly following Michael Schumacher's crash at Silverstone – as a worthwhile alternative.

However the decision to continue with Coulthard was in no way a second choice. On balance it was felt that David had shown himself to be an excellent team player with a nicely balanced personality. He was a hugely popular promotional asset in the eyes of Mercedes-Benz. Ultimately, the benefits of continuity and stability were preferred to the excitement – and the possibility of personality clashes – involved in recruiting free-thinking Irvine.

---

from the team's physiotherapist in order to ease the aches and pains that inevitably build up in an environment where cornering loads can impose up to 4.5G on their bodies. Throughout the weekend there is simply not a second to spare for either of them, in or out of the car.

'Everything is planned and organised right down to the last detail,' said Hakkinen. 'From Thursday right through to Sunday night, and not just when you are in the car. Every day you have meetings with the engineers and mechanics, press work, sponsor appearances, and there are still people who sometimes think that Mika never comes out of the garage or motorhome.

'The reality, of course, is that you have no time to come out. It is hard work, a very serious business indeed. F1 is a mind game, no question about it.'

Prior to qualifying, both drivers will ensure that they have some time alone to get their minds firmly into gear and cleared of any extraneous thoughts. Hakkinen will mentally run through all his gearchange and turn-in points. For the whole team, qualifying is an hour in which the drivers and cars come first and is possibly the most exciting moment of the weekend.

'After a good qualifying session, the boys are over the moon,' reflects Steve Hallam. Celebrating pole position became something of a McLaren habit in 1999 with Mika qualifying fastest in the first five races of the season. Often the Finn will time his quickest run late in the session, frequently entering his final lap only seconds before the chequered flag is shown. It usually works because Mika is so calm, confident and absolutely sure of his own judgement.

Most strategy decisions are made prior to the race start

Underpinning the McLaren drivers' weekends is an on-going programme of physical preparation. Both drivers train on Thursday, Friday and Saturday evening and carry out a lot of mobility exercises – just loosening up – on Sundays. They both follow what is described as 'a fairly standard sports diet' with around 60 per cent carbohydrates, proteins and a low-fat content. They both try to avoid eating within two hours of strapping themselves into the cockpit and try to get at least eight hours' sleep each night.

Inevitably, the pressure is stepped up on race day. The paddock is overflowing with fans, corporate guests and journalists, all of whom are trying to snatch a second of the drivers' time. But the McLaren team has built up a huge data bank of experience when it comes to keeping focused on the job in hand.

At 8 o'clock on race morning Adrian Newey and his race engineers will meet their opposite numbers from Ilmor to discuss engine settings, half an hour after which they will be joined by the two drivers who will be briefed on the forthcoming half-hour warm-up session. That takes place from 9.30, during which final assessment of the race tyres is carried out and the spare car checked out for a few laps by whichever driver has been allotted it for this particular weekend.

There is a quick technical debrief after this session and with just under two hours left to run there is a final race strategy meeting where a decision will be confirmed as to how many refuelling stops will be made during the course of the race.

With half an hour to go the cars take up their positions on the grid and the pit lane finally closes with 15 minutes left to run. Even the most highly experienced and seasoned team member feels his heart beating a little faster as the cars accelerate away on their parade lap before taking up their final positions on the grid. The lights on the starting gantry over the pits are then illuminated one by one, then extinguished together and the pack is off towards the first corner in a frenzied multi-coloured blur, an overwhelming crash of sound and a cloud of dust that lingers in the air for some time thereafter.

Judging when a pit stop should be made involves balancing the all-up weight of a car with the amount of fuel necessary to cover the planned

Secrecy is all: Covers over the nose sections of the McLaren MP4/13s at the 1998 British Grand Prix – and over the front chassis bulkhead of the MP4/14 at Monaco, 1999.
(Formula One Pictures)

distance while at the same time taking into account tyre wear considerations. Yet although the McLaren personnel may think on their feet in order to change the strategy to accommodate unexpected developments as the race unfolds, most of the decisions have been made prior to the start. Ron Dennis and his colleagues have huge confidence in their drivers' ability to get things right once the action starts.

Changes in track temperature may adversely affect tyre performance, which causes a handling imbalance. If this is reported over the radio link by Mika or David, changes in pressure may have to be made to those tyres waiting to be fitted to the car at the next refuelling stop.

All competitors have a refuelling 'window' – a handful of laps during which they can make a scheduled stop. This is worked into the game plan to give the driver a degree of flexibility, possibly to take advantage of a close rival pitting earlier and enabling the other car to stay out slightly longer in the hope of gaining a fractional track advantage before making its own stop.

Yet if one of the McLaren-Mercedes gets stuck in slow traffic – or looks as though it is closing on the tails of back markers quite quickly – it may be the best choice to bring that car in slightly earlier than originally planned. Such heavy traffic caused David Coulthard to lose his chance of winning the 1999 San Marino Grand Prix at Imola, but

Coulthard signs for his fans at the 1996 Italian Grand Prix. (Formula One Pictures)

the McLaren management neverthe-less believes that he was right not to be panicked into changing his strategy 'on the hoof'.

Finally the decision is made and the car concerned comes into view in the pit lane. The driver has to have his wits about him at this stage in the race, for not only must he remember to engage his car's pit lane speed limiter, he also has to concentrate on making the swiftest and most accurate approach to his pit, stopping precisely adjacent to the mechanics who are waiting with the four replacement tyres. Sometimes this goes slightly wrong, as when David overshot his pit crew at his first refu-elling stop during the 1999 Spanish Grand Prix. He wasn't far out of line, and the lads were able to complete their tasks without too much drama, but the slight delay in offering up the wheels and refuelling nozzle cost the Scot an extra 4 seconds.

In the 8 seconds or so in which the car is at rest, the pit crew get the job completed. The driver keeps his right foot firmly on the brake and, within a second of the car stopping, the jacks go under the front and rear of the car. Simultaneously, one mechanic per wheel attaches the compressed-air wheel-gun to the central nut locating that wheel on its hub.

By the time a second mechanic has physically removed the wheel, 1.6 seconds will have passed since the car stopped. A third mechanic on each corner fits a replacement wheel and tyre only 2.2 seconds into the stop, the wheels are fully tightened in 4.2 seconds and the locking pins posi-tioned in 5.2 seconds.

Tech chief Adrian Newey, deep in thought. (Formula One Pictures)

While this work is proceeding, two more mechanics are in control of the refuelling line that attaches to a quick-release connection on the side of the fuel cell, with a third operating the refuelling rig itself.

This task is completed 7.7 seconds after the car first rolled to a halt and the refuelling hose is duly removed. The refuelling rigs are supplied by the FIA – but paid for by the competing teams! – with the same controlled flow

How it's supposed to end: Hakkinen celebrates and, from left, Mansour Ojjeh, Ron Dennis and Mika Hakkinen are all smiles after the Finn's victory in the 1998 Spanish Grand Prix. (Formula One Pictures)

rate for competitors, which allows reasonably accurate calculations for consumption purposes. Just occasionally there is a malfunction that perhaps prevents all the allotted fuel from entering the car, glitches of which strategic nightmares are made and as a result of which races are unexpectedly won and lost.

From the front of the car, chief mechanic Mike Negline keeps a watchful eye on the refuelling process, only signalling the driver back into the race when he is satisfied that all the various tasks have been completed totally by the book.

Hopefully for the McLaren squad, by the time the chequered flag flutters to mark the end of the race, one or other of their cars will pass it first to notch up yet another race victory. And prefer-

ably a 1–2. 'The whole point of the weekend is winning the race,' says Mike Negline, adequately reflecting Ron Dennis's admission that if he wakes up on Monday morning and realises his team didn't win the previous afternoon, he feels an almost physical sense of pain.

'Just remember, being second is first of the losers.' Those memorable words were first uttered by Dennis when he came upon the Peugeot engineers celebrating after Martin Brundle's second place in the 1994 Monaco Grand Prix.

At the time, it seemed a touch insensitive. 'We knew what he meant,' said Brundle, 'but there is a time and a place.' Cruel it may have seemed. Yet Dennis would just regard himself as being starkly honest. And true to the burning sense of ambition that suffuses the entire McLaren-Mercedes team from top to bottom.

Appendix 1

McLaren – race results

Key to abbreviations:
R – retired; A – did not appear at meeting; S – did not start; Q – did not qualify; D – disqualified; W – withdrawn; § – did not complete enough of race distance to be classified; * – classified but not running at finish. Numbers relate to finishing position

1966
McLaren-Ford M2B (unless otherwise stated)

22 May MONACO, Monte Carlo
   C. Amon   A
   B. McLaren   R
12 Jun BELGIAN, Spa
   B. McLaren, Serenissima   S
   C. Amon   A
3 Jul FRENCH, Reims
   B. McLaren, Serenissima   A
16 Jul BRITISH, Brands Hatch
   B. McLaren, Serenissima   6
   C. Amon   A
7 Aug GERMAN, Nurburgring
   B. McLaren   W
4 Sep ITALIAN, Monza
   B. McLaren   W
   C. Amon   W
2 Oct US, Watkins Glen
   B. McLaren   5
23 Oct MEXICAN, Mexico City
   B. McLaren   R

1967
McLaren M4B-BRM V8 (Monaco-Holland); McLaren M5A-BRM V12 (Canada-Mexico)

7 May MONACO, Monte Carlo
   B. McLaren   4
4 Jun DUTCH, Zandvoort
   B. McLaren   R
27 Aug CANADIAN, Mosport Park
   B. McLaren   7
10 Sep ITALIAN, Monza
   B. McLaren   R
1 Oct US, Watkins Glen
   B. McLaren   R
22 Oct MEXICAN, Mexico City
   B. McLaren   R

1968
McLaren M5A-BRM V12 (South Africa); McLaren M7A-Cosworth DFV (Spain-Mexico); McLaren M5A-BRM V12 (J. Bonnier, Italy, US-Mexico)

1 Jan SOUTH AFRICAN, Kyalami
   D. Hulme   5
12 May SPANISH, Jarama
   D. Hulme   2
   B. McLaren   R
26 May MONACO, Monte Carlo
   D. Hulme   5
   B. McLaren   R
9 Jun BELGIAN, Spa
   B. McLaren   1
   D. Hulme   R
23 Jun DUTCH, Zandvoort
   D. Hulme   R
   B. McLaren   R

7 Jul FRENCH, Rouen
   D. Hulme   5
   B. McLaren   8
20 Jul BRITISH, Brands Hatch
   D. Hulme   4
   B. McLaren   7
4 Aug GERMAN, Nurburgring
   D. Hulme   7
   B. McLaren   13
8 Sep ITALIAN, Monza
   D. Hulme   1
   B. McLaren   R
   J. Bonnier   6
22 Sep CANADIAN, Ste Jovite
   D. Hulme   1
   B. McLaren   2
   D. Gurney   R
6 Oct US, Watkins Glen
   D. Hulme   R
   B. McLaren   6
   D. Gurney   4
   J. Bonnier   14§
3 Nov MEXICAN, Mexico City
   D. Hulme   R
   B. McLaren   2
   D. Gurney   R
   J. Bonnier   S

1969
McLaren-Cosworth; chassis type given

1 Mar SOUTH AFRICAN, Kyalami
   D. Hulme, M7A   3
   B. McLaren, M7A   5
   B. van Rooyen, M7A   R
4 May SPANISH, Montjuich
   D. Hulme, M7A   4
   B. McLaren, M7C   2

18 May MONACO, Monte Carlo
D. Hulme, M7A 6
B. McLaren, M7C 5
21 Jun DUTCH, Zandvoort
B. McLaren, M7C R
D. Hulme, M7A 4
V. Elford, M7A 10
6 Jul FRENCH, Clermont Ferrand
D. Hulme, M7A 8
B. McLaren, M7C 4
V. Elford, M7A 5
19 Jul BRITISH, Silverstone
D. Hulme, M7A R
B. McLaren, M7C 3
V. Elford, M7A 6
D. Bell, M9A 4WD R
3 Aug GERMAN, Nurburgring
D. Hulme, M7A R
B. McLaren, M7C 3
V. Elford, M7A R
7 Sep ITALIAN, Monza
D. Hulme, M7A 7
B. McLaren, M7C 4
20 Sep CANADIAN, Mosport Park
B. McLaren, M7C 5
D. Hulme, M7A R
V. Elford, M7A A
5 Oct US, Watkins Glen
D. Hulme, M7A R
B. McLaren, M7C S
19 Oct MEXICAN, Mexico City
D. Hulme, M7A 1
B. McLaren, M7A R

1970
McLaren-Cosworth; chassis type given

7 Mar SOUTH AFRICAN, Kyalami
B. McLaren, M14A R
D. Hulme, M14A 2
J. Surtees, M7C R
19 Apr SPANISH, Jarama
D. Hulme, M14A R
J. Surtees, M7C R
B. McLaren, M14A 2
A. de Adamich, M7D-Alfa V8 Q
10 May MONACO, Monte Carlo
A. de Adamich, M7D-Alfa V8 Q
D. Hulme, M14A 4
B. McLaren, M14A R
J. Surtees, M7C R
7 Jun BELGIAN, Spa
B. McLaren, M14A W
D. Hulme, M14A W
A. de Adamich, M7D-Alfa V8 W
J. Surtees, M7C W
21 Jun DUTCH, Zandvoort
P. Gethin, M14A R
A. de Adamich, M14D-Alfa V8 Q
D. Gurney, M14A R
5 Jul FRENCH, Clermont Ferrand
A. de Adamich, M7D-Alfa V8 15
D. Gurney, M14A 6
D. Hulme, M14A 4
J. Surtees, M7C A

19 Jul BRITISH, Brands Hatch
D. Hulme, M14A 3
D. Gurney, M7A R
A. de Adamich, M7D-Alfa V8 S
P. Gethin, M7A A
T. Taylor, M7C A
J. Bonnier, M7C A
2 Aug GERMAN, Hockenheim
D. Hulme, M14A 3
A. de Adamich, M14D-Alfa V8 Q
P. Gethin, M14A R
16 Aug AUSTRIAN, Osterreichring
D. Hulme, M14A R
A. de Adamich, M14D-Alfa V8 12
P. Gethin, M14A 10
6 Sep ITALIAN, Monza
D. Hulme, M14A 4
P. Gethin, M14A 9§
A. de Adamich, M14D-Alfa V8 8
G. Galli, M7D Q
20 Sep CANADIAN, Ste Jovite
D. Hulme, M14A R
P. Gethin, M14A 6
A. de Adamich, M14D-Alfa V8 R
4 Oct US, Watkins Glen
D. Hulme, M14A 7
P. Gethin, M14A 14
A. de Adamich, M14D-Alfa V8 Q
J. Bonnier, M7C R
25 Oct MEXICAN, Mexico City
D. Hulme, M14A 3
P. Gethin, M14A R
J. Bonnier, M7C A

1971
McLaren-Cosworth; chassis type given

6 Mar SOUTH AFRICAN, Kyalami
D. Hulme, M19A 6
P. Gethin, M14A R
J. Bonnier, M7C R
18 Apr SPANISH, Montjuich
D. Hulme, M19A 5
P. Gethin, M14A 8
J. Bonnier, M7C A
23 May MONACO, Monte Carlo
D. Hulme, M19A 4
P. Gethin, M14A R
20 Jun DUTCH, Zandvoort
D. Hulme, M19A 12
P. Gethin, M19A 15§
4 Jul FRENCH, Ricard
D. Hulme, M19A R
P. Gethin, M19A 9
17 Jul BRITISH, Silverstone
D. Hulme, M19A R
P. Gethin, M19A R
J. Oliver, M14A R
1 Aug GERMAN, Nurburgring
D. Hulme, M19A R
J. Oliver, M14A A
P. Gethin, M19A R

15 Aug AUSTRIAN, Osterreichring
D. Hulme, M19A R
J. Oliver, M19A 9
J. Bonnier, M7C S
5 Sep ITALIAN, Monza
J. Oliver, M14A 7
J. Bonnier, M7C 10
19 Sep CANADIAN, Mosport Park
D. Hulme, M19A 4
M. Donohue, M19A 3
3 Oct US, Watkins Glen
D. Hulme, M19A R
J. Bonnier, M7C 16
D. Hobbs, M19A 10

1972
McLaren-Cosworth; chassis type given

23 Jan ARGENTINE, Buenos Aires
D. Hulme, M19A 2
P. Revson, M19A R
4 Mar SOUTH AFRICAN, Kyalami
D. Hulme, M19A 1
P. Revson, M19A 3
1 May SPANISH, Jarama
D. Hulme, M19A R
P. Revson, M19A 5
14 May MONACO, Monte Carlo
D. Hulme, M19C 15
B. Redman, M19A 5
4 Jun BELGIAN, Nivelles
D. Hulme, M19C 3
P. Revson, M19A 7
2 Jul FRENCH, Clermont Ferrand
D. Hulme, M19C 7
B. Redman, M19A 9
15 Jul BRITISH, Brands Hatch
D. Hulme, M19C 5
P. Revson, M19A 3
B. Redman, M19A A
30 Jul GERMAN, Nurburgring
D. Hulme, M19C R
B. Redman, M19A 5
13 Aug AUSTRIAN, Osterreichring
D. Hulme, M19C 2
P. Revson, M19C 3
10 Sep ITALIAN, Monza
D. Hulme, M19C 3
P. Revson, M19C 4
24 Sep CANADIAN, Mosport Park
D. Hulme, M19C 3
P. Revson, M19C 2
8 Oct US, Watkins Glen
D. Hulme, M19C 3
P. Revson, M19C R
J. Scheckter, M19A 9

1973

McLaren-Cosworth M19C (Argentina-Brazil; Revson and Scheckter, Spain-US); McLaren-Cosworth M23 (Spain-US, Hulme, South Africa)

28 Jan ARGENTINE, Buenos Aires
D. Hulme	5
P. Revson	8

11 Feb BRAZILIAN, Interlagos
D. Hulme	3
P. Revson	R

3 Mar SOUTH AFRICAN, Kyalami
D. Hulme	5
P. Revson	2
J. Scheckter	9

29 Apr SPANISH, Montjuich
D. Hulme	6
P. Revson	4

20 May BELGIAN, Zolder
D. Hulme	7
P. Revson	R

3 Jun MONACO, Monte Carlo
D. Hulme	6
P. Revson	5

17 Jun SWEDISH, Anderstorp
D. Hulme	1
P. Revson	7

1 Jul FRENCH, Ricard
D. Hulme	8
J. Scheckter	R

14 Jul BRITISH, Silverstone
D. Hulme	3
P. Revson	1
J. Scheckter	R

29 Jul DUTCH, Zandvoort
D. Hulme	R
P. Revson	4

5 Aug GERMAN, Nurburgring
D. Hulme	12
P. Revson	9
J. Ickx	3

19 Aug AUSTRIAN, Osterreichring
D. Hulme	8
P. Revson	R

9 Sep ITALIAN, Monza
D. Hulme	15
P. Revson	3

23 Sep CANADIAN, Mosport Park
J. Scheckter	R
D. Hulme	13
P. Revson	1

7 Oct US, Watkins Glen
J. Scheckter	R
D. Hulme	4
P. Revson	5

1974

McLaren-Cosworth M23

13 Jan ARGENTINE, Buenos Aires
E. Fittipaldi	10
D. Hulme	1
M. Hailwood	4

27 Jan BRAZILIAN, Interlagos
E. Fittipaldi	1
D. Hulme	12
M. Hailwood	5

30 Mar SOUTH AFRICAN, Kyalami
E. Fittipaldi	7
D. Hulme	9
D. Charlton	19
M. Hailwood	3

28 Apr SPANISH, Jarama
E. Fittipaldi	3
D. Hulme	6
M. Hailwood	9

12 May BELGIAN, Nivelles
E. Fittipaldi	1
D. Hulme	6
M. Hailwood	7

26 May MONACO, Monte Carlo
E. Fittipaldi	5
D. Hulme	R
M. Hailwood	R

9 Jun SWEDISH, Anderstorp
E. Fittipaldi	4
D. Hulme	R
M. Hailwood	R

23 Jun DUTCH, Zandvoort
E. Fittipaldi	3
D. Hulme	R
M. Hailwood	4

7 Jul FRENCH, Dijon
E. Fittipaldi	R
D. Hulme	6
M. Hailwood	7

20 Jul BRITISH, Brands Hatch
E. Fittipaldi	2
D. Hulme	7
M. Hailwood	R

4 Aug GERMAN, Nurburgring
E. Fittipaldi	R
D. Hulme	R
M. Hailwood	R

18 Aug AUSTRIAN, Osterreichring
E. Fittipaldi	18§
D. Hulme	2
D. Hobbs	7

8 Sep ITALIAN, Monza
E. Fittipaldi	2
D. Hulme	6
D. Hobbs	9

22 Sep CANADIAN, Mosport Park
E. Fittipaldi	1
D. Hulme	6
J. Mass	16

6 Oct US, Watkins Glen
E. Fittipaldi	4
D. Hulme	R
J. Mass	7

1975

McLaren-Cosworth M23

12 Jan ARGENTINE, Buenos Aires
E. Fittipaldi	1
J. Mass	14

26 Jan BRAZILIAN, Interlagos
E. Fittipaldi	2
J. Mass	3

1 Mar SOUTH AFRICAN, Kyalami
E. Fittipaldi	19§
J. Mass	6
D. Charlton	14

27 Apr SPANISH, Montjuich
E. Fittipaldi	S
J. Mass	1

11 May MONACO, Monte Carlo
E. Fittipaldi	2
J. Mass	6

25 May BELGIAN, Zolder
E. Fittipaldi	7
J. Mass	R

8 Jun SWEDISH, Anderstorp
E. Fittipaldi	8
J. Mass	R

22 Jun DUTCH, Zandvoort
E. Fittipaldi	R
J. Mass	R

6 Jul FRENCH, Ricard
E. Fittipaldi	4
J. Mass	3

19 Jul BRITISH, Silverstone
E. Fittipaldi	1
J. Mass	7

3 Aug GERMAN, Nurburgring
E. Fittipaldi	R
J. Mass	R

17 Aug AUSTRIAN, Osterreichring
E. Fittipaldi	9
J. Mass	4

7 Sep ITALIAN, Monza
E. Fittipaldi	2
J. Mass	R

5 Oct US, Watkins Glen
E. Fittipaldi	2
J. Mass	3

1976

McLaren-Cosworth M23; McLaren-Cosworth M26 (Mass only, Holland-Italy)

25 Jan BRAZILIAN, Interlagos
J. Hunt	R
J. Mass	6

6 Mar SOUTH AFRICAN, Kyalami
J. Hunt	2
J. Mass	3

28 Mar US WEST, Long Beach
J. Hunt	R
J. Mass	5

2 May SPANISH, Jarama
J. Hunt	1
J. Mass	R

16 May BELGIAN, Zolder
J. Hunt	R
J. Mass	6

23 May MONACO, Monte Carlo
J. Hunt	R
J. Mass	5

13 Jun SWEDISH, Anderstorp
J. Hunt 5
J. Mass 11
4 Jul FRENCH, Ricard
J. Hunt 1
J. Mass 15
18 Jul BRITISH, Brands Hatch
J. Hunt D
J. Mass R
1 Aug GERMAN, Nurburgring
J. Hunt 1
J. Mass 3
15 Aug AUSTRIAN, Osterreichring
J. Hunt 4
J. Mass 7
29 Aug DUTCH, Zandvoort
J. Hunt 1
J. Mass 9
12 Sep ITALIAN, Monza
J. Hunt R
J. Mass R
3 Oct CANADIAN, Mosport Park
J. Hunt 1
J. Mass 5
10 Oct US EAST, Watkins Glen
J. Hunt 1
J. Mass 4
17 Oct JAPANESE, Fuji
J. Hunt 3
J. Mass R

1977

McLaren-Cosworth M23; McLaren-Cosworth M26 (Hunt, Spain-Japan; Mass, Britain-Japan)

9 Jan ARGENTINE, Buenos Aires
J. Hunt R
J. Mass R
23 Jan BRAZILIAN, Interlagos
J. Hunt 2
J. Mass R
5 Mar SOUTH AFRICAN, Kyalami
J. Hunt 4
J. Mass 5
3 Apr US WEST, Long Beach
J. Hunt 7
J. Mass R
8 May SPANISH, Jarama
J. Hunt R
J. Mass 4
E. de Villota 13
22 May MONACO, Monte Carlo
J. Hunt R
J. Mass 4
5 Jun BELGIAN, Zolder
J. Hunt 7
J. Mass R
B. Lunger S
E. de Villota Q
19 Jun SWEDISH, Anderstorp
J. Hunt 12
J. Mass 2
B. Lunger 11
E. de Villota Q

3 Jul FRENCH, Dijon
J. Hunt 3
J. Mass 9
B. Lunger Q
E. de Villota A
16 Jul BRITISH, Silverstone
J. Hunt 1
J. Mass 4
B. Lunger 13
E. de Villota Q
G. Villeneuve 11
31 Jul GERMAN, Hockenheim
J. Hunt R
J. Mass R
B. Lunger R
E. de Villota Q
14 Aug AUSTRIAN, Osterreichring
J. Hunt R
J. Mass 6
B. Lunger 10
E. de Villota R
28 Aug DUTCH, Zandvoort
J. Hunt R
J. Mass R
B. Lunger 9
11 Sep ITALIAN, Monza
J. Hunt R
J. Mass 4
B. Giacomelli R
B. Lunger R
E. de Villota Q
2 Oct US EAST, Watkins Glen
J. Hunt 1
J. Mass R
B. Lunger 10
9 Oct CANADIAN, Mosport Park
J. Hunt R
J. Mass 3
B. Lunger 11
23 Oct JAPANESE, Fuji
J. Hunt 1
J. Mass R

1978

McLaren-Cosworth M26 (unless otherwise stated)

15 Jan ARGENTINE, Buenos Aires
J. Hunt 4
P. Tambay 6
B. Lunger, M23 13
29 Jan BRAZILIAN, Rio
J. Hunt R
P. Tambay R
B. Lunger, M23 R
4 Mar SOUTH AFRICAN, Kyalami
J. Hunt R
P. Tambay R
B. Lunger, M23 11
2 Apr US WEST, Long Beach
J. Hunt R
P. Tambay 12
B. Lunger, M23 Q

7 May MONACO, Monte Carlo
J. Hunt R
P. Tambay 7
B. Lunger Q
21 May BELGIAN, Zolder
J. Hunt R
P. Tambay A
B. Lunger 7
B. Giacomelli 8
4 Jun SPANISH, Jarama
J. Hunt 6
P. Tambay R
E. de Villota, M23 Q
B. Lunger Q
17 Jun SWEDISH, Anderstorp
J. Hunt 8
P. Tambay 4
B. Lunger Q
1 Jul FRENCH, Ricard
J. Hunt 3
P. Tambay 9
B. Lunger R
B. Giacomelli R
16 Jul BRITISH, Brands Hatch
J. Hunt R
P. Tambay 6
B. Lunger 8
B. Giacomelli 7
T. Trimmer, M23 Q
30 Jul GERMAN, Hockenheim
J. Hunt D
P. Tambay R
13 Aug AUSTRIAN, Osterreichring
J. Hunt R
P. Tambay R
N. Piquet, M23 R
B. Lunger 8
27 Aug DUTCH, Zandvoort
J. Hunt 10
P. Tambay 9
N. Piquet, M23 R
B. Lunger R
B. Giacomelli R
10 Sep ITALIAN, Monza
J. Hunt R
P. Tambay 5
N. Piquet, M23 9
B. Lunger R
1 Oct US EAST, Watkins Glen
J. Hunt 7
P. Tambay 6
8 Oct CANADIAN, Montreal
J. Hunt R
P. Tambay 8

1979

McLaren-Cosworth M26 (Tambay, Belgium); McLaren-Cosworth M28 (Watson, Argentina-France; Tambay, Argentina-Spain, Monaco-Britain); McLaren-Cosworth M29 (Watson, Britain-US; Tambay, Germany-US)

21 Jan ARGENTINE, Buenos Aires
J. Watson	3
P. Tambay	R

4 Feb BRAZIL, Interlagos
J. Watson	8
P. Tambay	R

3 Mar SOUTH AFRICAN, Kyalami
J. Watson	R
P. Tambay	10

8 Apr US WEST, Long Beach
J. Watson	R
P. Tambay	R

29 Apr SPANISH, Jarama
J. Watson	R
P. Tambay	13

13 May BELGIAN, Zolder
J. Watson	6
P. Tambay	Q

27 May MONACO, Monte Carlo
J. Watson	4
P. Tambay	Q

1 Jul FRENCH, Dijon
J. Watson	11
P. Tambay	10

14 Jul BRITISH, Silverstone
J. Watson	4
P. Tambay	7

29 Jul GERMAN, Hockenheim
J. Watson	5
P. Tambay	R

12 Aug AUSTRIAN, Osterreichring
J. Watson	9
P. Tambay	10

26 Aug DUTCH, Zandvoort
J. Watson	R
P. Tambay	R

9 Sep ITALIAN, Monza
J. Watson	R
P. Tambay	R

30 Sep CANADIAN, Montreal
J. Watson	6
P. Tambay	R

7 Oct US EAST, Watkins Glen
J. Watson	6
P. Tambay	R

1980

McLaren-Cosworth M29 (Argentina-Austria; Watson(Holland-US); McLaren-Cosworth M30 (Prost, Holland-US)

13 Jan ARGENTINE, Buenos Aires
J. Watson	R
A. Prost	6

27 Jan BRAZILIAN, Interlagos
J. Watson	11
A. Prost	5

1 Mar SOUTH AFRICAN, Kyalami
J. Watson	11
A. Prost	S

30 Mar US WEST, Long Beach
J. Watson	4
S. South	Q

4 May BELGIAN, Zolder
J. Watson	13§
A. Prost	R

18 May MONACO, Monte Carlo
J. Watson	Q
A. Prost	R

1 Jun SPANISH, Jarama
J. Watson	R
A. Prost	R

29 Jun FRENCH, Ricard
J. Watson	7
A. Prost	R

13 Jul BRITISH, Brands Hatch
J. Watson	8
A. Prost	6

10 Aug GERMAN, Hockenheim
J. Watson	R
A. Prost	11

17 Aug AUSTRIAN, Osterreichring
J. Watson	R
A. Prost	7

31 Aug DUTCH, Zandvoort
J. Watson	R
A. Prost	6

14 Sep ITALIAN, Monza
J. Watson	R
A. Prost	7

29 Sep CANADIAN, Montreal
J. Watson	4
A. Prost	R

5 Oct US EAST, Watkins Glen
J. Watson	12§
A. Prost	S

1981

McLaren-Cosworth M29 (South Africa-Brazil; de Cesaris, Argentina-Belgium); McLaren-Cosworth MP4 (Watson, Argentina-US; de Cesaris (Monaco-US)

15 Mar US WEST, Long Beach
J. Watson	R
A. de Cesaris	R

29 Mar BRAZILIAN, Rio
J. Watson	8
A. de Cesaris	R

12 Apr ARGENTINE, Buenos Aires
J. Watson	R
A. de Cesaris	11

3 May SAN MARINO, Imola
J. Watson	10
A. de Cesaris	6

17 May BELGIAN, Zolder
J. Watson	7
A. de Cesaris	R

31 May MONACO, Monte Carlo
J. Watson	R
A. de Cesaris	R

21 Jun SPANISH, Jarama
J. Watson	3
A. de Cesaris	R

5 Jul FRENCH, Dijon
J. Watson	2
A. de Cesaris	11

18 Jul BRITISH, Silverstone
J. Watson	1
A. de Cesaris	R

2 Aug GERMAN, Hockenheim
J. Watson	6
A. de Cesaris	R

16 Aug AUSTRIAN, Osterreichring
J. Watson	6
A. de Cesaris	8

30 Aug DUTCH, Zandvoort
J. Watson	R
A. de Cesaris	S

13 Sep ITALIAN, Monza
J. Watson	R
A. de Cesaris	7

27 Sep CANADIAN, Montreal
J. Watson	2
A. de Cesaris	R

17 Oct US, Las Vegas
J. Watson	7
A. de Cesaris	12

1982

McLaren-Cosworth MP4

23 Jan SOUTH AFRICAN, Kyalami
J. Watson	6
N. Lauda	4

21 Mar BRAZILIAN, Rio
J. Watson	2
N. Lauda	R

4 Apr US WEST, Long Beach
J. Watson	6
N. Lauda	1

25 Apr SAN MARINO, Imola
Team entries withdrawn	

9 May BELGIAN, Zolder
J. Watson	1
N. Lauda	D

23 May MONACO, Monte Carlo
J. Watson	R
N. Lauda	R

6 Jun US, Detroit
J. Watson	1
N. Lauda	R

13 Jun CANADIAN, Montreal
J. Watson	3
N. Lauda	R

3 Jul DUTCH, Zandvoort
J. Watson	9
N. Lauda	4

18 Jul BRITISH, Brands Hatch
J. Watson	R
N. Lauda	1

25 Jul FRENCH, Ricard
J. Watson — R
N. Lauda — 8
8 Aug GERMAN, Hockenheim
J. Watson — R
N. Lauda — S
15 Aug AUSTRIAN, Osterreichring
J. Watson — R
N. Lauda — 5
29 Aug SWISS, Dijon
J. Watson — 13
N. Lauda — 3
12 Sep ITALIAN, Monza
J. Watson — 4
N. Lauda — R
25 Sep US, Las Vegas
J. Watson — 2
N. Lauda — R

1983
McLaren-Cosworth MP4/1C (Brazil-Austria; Watson, Holland); McLaren-TAG MP4/1E (Holland-South Africa)

13 Mar BRAZILIAN, Rio
J. Watson — R
N. Lauda — 3
27 Mar US WEST, Long Beach
J. Watson — 1
N. Lauda — 2
17 Apr FRENCH, Ricard
J. Watson — R
N. Lauda — R
30 Apr SAN MARINO, Imola
J. Watson — 5
N. Lauda — R
15 May MONACO, Monte Carlo
J. Watson — Q
N. Lauda — Q
22 May BELGIAN, Spa
J. Watson — R
N. Lauda — R
5 Jun US, Detroit
J. Watson — 3
N. Lauda — R
12 Jun CANADIAN, Montreal
J. Watson — 6
N. Lauda — R
16 Jul BRITISH, Silverstone
J. Watson — 9
N. Lauda — 6
7 Aug GERMAN, Hockenheim
J. Watson — 5
N. Lauda — D
14 Aug AUSTRIAN, Osterreichring
J. Watson — 9
N. Lauda — 6
28 Aug DUTCH, Zandvoort
J. Watson — 3
N. Lauda — R
11 Sep ITALIAN, Monza
J. Watson — R
N. Lauda — R

25 Sep EUROPEAN, Brands Hatch
J. Watson — R
N. Lauda — R
15 Oct SOUTH AFRICAN, Kyalami
J. Watson — D
N. Lauda — 11*

1984
McLaren-TAG MP4/2

25 Mar, BRAZILIAN, Rio
A. Prost — 1
N. Lauda — R
7 Apr SOUTH AFRICAN, Kyalami
A. Prost — 2
N. Lauda — 1
29 Apr BELGIAN, Zolder
A. Prost — R
N. Lauda — R
6 May SAN MARINO, Imola
A. Prost — 1
N. Lauda — R
20 May FRENCH, Dijon
A. Prost — 7
N. Lauda — 1
3 Jun MONACO, Monte Carlo
A. Prost — 1
N. Lauda — R
17 Jun CANADIAN, Montreal
A. Prost — 3
N. Lauda — 2
24 Jun US, Detroit
A. Prost — 4
N. Lauda — R
8 Jul US, Dallas
A. Prost — R
N. Lauda — R
22 Jul BRITISH, Brands Hatch
A. Prost — R
N. Lauda — 1
5 Aug GERMAN, Hockenheim
A. Prost — 1
N. Lauda — 2
19 Aug AUSTRIAN, Osterreichring
A. Prost — R
N. Lauda — 1
26 Aug DUTCH, Zandvoort
A. Prost — 1
N. Lauda — 2
9 Sep ITALIAN, Monza
A. Prost — R
N. Lauda — 1
7 Oct EUROPEAN, Nurburgring
A. Prost — 1
N. Lauda — 4
21 Oct PORTUGUESE, Estoril
A. Prost — 1
N. Lauda — 2

1985
McLaren-TAG MP4/2B

7 Apr BRAZILIAN, Rio
N. Lauda — R
A. Prost — 1

21 Apr PORTUGUESE, Estoril
N. Lauda — R
A. Prost — R
5 May SAN MARINO, Imola
N. Lauda — 4
A. Prost — D
19 May MONACO, Monte Carlo
N. Lauda — R
A. Prost — 1
16 Jun CANADIAN, Montreal
N. Lauda — R
A. Prost — 3
23 Jun US, Detroit
N. Lauda — R
A. Prost — R
7 Jul FRENCH, Ricard
N. Lauda — R
A. Prost — 3
21 Jul BRITISH, Silverstone
N. Lauda — R
A. Prost — 1
4 Aug GERMAN, Nurburgring
N. Lauda — 5
A. Prost — 2
18 Aug AUSTRIAN, Osterreichring
N. Lauda — R
A. Prost — 1
25 Aug DUTCH, Zandvoort
N. Lauda — 1
A. Prost — 2
8 Sep ITALIAN, Monza
N. Lauda — R
A. Prost — 1
15 Sep BELGIAN, Spa
N. Lauda — S
A. Prost — 3
6 Oct EUROPEAN, Brands Hatch
J. Watson — 7
A. Prost — 4
19 Oct SOUTH AFRICAN, Kyalami
N. Lauda — R
A. Prost — 3
3 Nov AUSTRALIAN, Adelaide
N. Lauda — R
A. Prost — R

1986
McLaren-TAG MP4/2C

23 Mar BRAZILIAN, Rio
A. Prost — R
K. Rosberg — R
13 Apr SPANISH, Jerez
A. Prost — 3
K. Rosberg — 4
27 Apr SAN MARINO, Imola
A. Prost — 1
K. Rosberg — 5*
11 May MONACO, Monte Carlo
A. Prost — 1
K. Rosberg — 2
25 May BELGIAN, Spa
A. Prost — 6
K. Rosberg — R

15 Jun CANADIAN, Montreal
A. Prost 2
K. Rosberg 4
22 Jun US, Detroit
A. Prost 3
K. Rosberg R
6 Jul FRENCH, Ricard
A. Prost 2
K. Rosberg 4
13 Jul BRITISH, Brands Hatch
A. Prost 3
K. Rosberg R
27 Jul GERMAN, Hockenheim
A. Prost 6*
K. Rosberg 5*
10 Aug HUNGARIAN, Hungaroring
A. Prost R
K. Rosberg R
17 Aug AUSTRIAN, Osterreichring
A. Prost 1
K. Rosberg 9*
7 Sep ITALIAN, Monza
A. Prost R
K. Rosberg 4
21 Sep PORTUGUESE, Estoril
A. Prost 2
K. Rosberg R
12 Oct MEXICAN, Mexico City
A. Prost 2
K. Rosberg R
26 Oct AUSTRALIAN, Adelaide
A. Prost 1
K. Rosberg R

1987
McLaren-TAG MP4/3

12 Apr BRAZILIAN, Rio
A. Prost 1
S. Johansson 3
3 May SAN MARINO, Imola
A. Prost R
S. Johansson 4
17 May, BELGIAN, Spa
A. Prost 1
S. Johansson 2
31 May MONACO, Monte Carlo
A. Prost 9*
S. Johansson R
21 Jun US, Detroit
A. Prost 3
S. Johansson 7
5 Jul FRENCH, Ricard
A. Prost 3
S. Johansson 8*
12 Jul BRITISH, Silverstone
A. Prost R
S. Johansson R
26 Jul GERMAN, Hockenheim
A. Prost 7*
S. Johansson 2
9 Aug HUNGARIAN, Hungaroring
A. Prost 3
S. Johansson R

16 Aug AUSTRIAN, Osterreichring
A. Prost 6
S. Johansson 7
6 Sep ITALIAN, Monza
A. Prost 15
S. Johansson 6
20 Sep PORTUGUESE, Estoril
A. Prost 1
S. Johansson 5
27 Sep SPANISH, Jerez
A. Prost 2
S. Johansson 3
18 Oct MEXICAN, Mexico City
A. Prost R
S. Johansson R
1 Nov JAPANESE, Suzuka
A. Prost 7
S. Johansson 3
15 Nov AUSTRALIAN, Adelaide
A. Prost R
S. Johansson R

1988
McLaren-Honda MP4/4

3 Apr BRAZILIAN, Rio
A. Prost 1
A. Senna R
1 May SAN MARINO, Imola
A. Prost 2
A. Senna 1
15 May MONACO, Monte Carlo
A. Prost 1
A. Senna R
29 May MEXICAN, Mexico City
A. Prost 1
A. Senna 2
12 Jun CANADIAN, Montreal
A. Prost 2
A. Senna 1
19 Jun US, Detroit
A. Prost 2
A. Senna 1
3 Jul FRENCH, Ricard
A. Prost 1
A. Senna 2
10 Jul BRITISH, Silverstone
A. Prost R
A. Senna 1
24 Jul GERMAN, Hockenheim
A. Prost 2
A. Senna 1
7 Aug HUNGARIAN, Hungaroring
A. Prost 2
A. Senna 1
28 Aug BELGIAN, Spa
A. Prost 2
A. Senna 1
11 Sep ITALIAN, Monza
A. Prost R
A. Senna 10*
25 Sep PORTUGUESE, Estoril
A. Prost 1
A. Senna 6

2 Oct SPANISH, Jerez
A. Prost 1
A. Senna 4
30 Oct JAPANESE, Suzuka
A. Prost 2
A. Senna 1
13 Nov AUSTRALIAN, Adelaide
A. Prost 1
A. Senna 2

1989
McLaren-Honda MP4/5

26 Mar BRAZILIAN, Rio
A. Senna 11
A. Prost 2
23 Apr SAN MARINO, Imola
A. Senna 1
A. Prost 2
7 May MONACO, Monte Carlo
A. Senna 1
A. Prost 2
28 May MEXICAN, Mexico City
A. Senna 1
A. Prost 5
4 Jun US, Phoenix
A. Senna R
A. Prost 1
18 Jun CANADIAN, Montreal
A. Senna 7*
A. Prost R
9 Jul FRENCH, Ricard
A. Senna R
A. Prost 1
16 Jul BRITISH, Silverstone
A. Senna R
A. Prost 1
30 Jul GERMAN, Hockenheim
A. Senna 1
A. Prost 2
13 Aug HUNGARIAN, Hungaroring
A. Senna 2
A. Prost 4
27 Aug BELGIAN, Spa
A. Senna 1
A. Prost 2
10 Sep ITALIAN, Monza
A. Senna R
A. Prost 1
24 Sep PORTUGUESE, Estoril
A. Senna R
A. Prost 2
1 Oct SPANISH, Jerez
A. Senna 1
A. Prost 3
22 Oct JAPANESE, Suzuka
A. Senna D
A. Prost R
5 Nov AUSTRALIAN, Adelaide
A. Senna R
A. Prost S

1990

McLaren-Honda MP4/5B

11 Mar US, Phoenix
A. Senna — 1
G. Berger — R

25 Mar BRAZILIAN, Interlagos
A. Senna — 3
G. Berger — 2

13 May SAN MARINO, Imola
A. Senna — R
G. Berger — 2

27 May MONACO, Monte Carlo
A. Senna — 1
G. Berger — 3

10 Jun CANADIAN, Montreal
A. Senna — 1
G. Berger — 4

24 Jun MEXICAN, Mexico City
A. Senna — 20*
G. Berger — 3

8 Jul FRENCH, Ricard
A. Senna — 3
G. Berger — 5

15 Jul BRITISH, Silverstone
A. Senna — 3
G. Berger — 14*

29 Jul GERMAN, Hockenheim
A. Senna — 1
G. Berger — 3

12 Aug HUNGARIAN, Hungaroring
A. Senna — 2
G. Berger — 16*

25 Aug BELGIAN, Spa
A. Senna — 1
G. Berger — 3

9 Sep ITALIAN, Monza
A. Senna — 1
G. Berger — 3

23 Sep PORTUGUESE, Estoril
A. Senna — 2
G. Berger — 4

30 Sep SPANISH, Jerez
A. Senna — R
G. Berger — R

21 Oct JAPANESE, Suzuka
A. Senna — R
G. Berger — R

4 Nov AUSTRALIAN, Adelaide
A. Senna — R
G. Berger — 4

1991

McLaren-Honda MP4/6

10 Mar US, Phoenix
A. Senna — 1
G. Berger — R

24 Mar BRAZILIAN, Interlagos
A. Senna — 1
G. Berger — 3

28 Apr SAN MARINO, Imola
A. Senna — 1
G. Berger — 2

12 May MONACO, Monte Carlo
A. Senna — 1
G. Berger — R

2 Jun CANADIAN, Montreal
A. Senna — R
G. Berger — R

16 Jun MEXICAN, Mexico City
A. Senna — 3
G. Berger — R

7 Jul FRENCH, Magny-Cours
A. Senna — 3
G. Berger — R

14 Jul BRITISH, Silverstone
A. Senna — 4*
G. Berger — 2

28 Jul GERMAN, Hockenheim
A. Senna — 7*
G. Berger — 4

11 Aug HUNGARIAN, Hungaroring
A. Senna — 1
G. Berger — 4

25 Aug BELGIAN, Spa
A. Senna — 1
G. Berger — 2

8 Sep ITALIAN, Monza
A. Senna — 2
G. Berger — 4

22 Sep PORTUGUESE, Estoril
A. Senna — 2
G. Berger — R

29 Sep SPANISH, Barcelona
A. Senna — 5
G. Berger — R

20 Oct JAPANESE, Suzuka
A. Senna — 2
G. Berger — 1

3 Nov AUSTRALIAN, Adelaide
A. Senna — 1
G. Berger — 3

1992

McLaren-Honda MP4/6B (South Africa-Mexico); McLaren-Honda MP4/7A (Brazil-Australia)

1 Mar SOUTH AFRICAN, Kyalami
A. Senna — 3
G. Berger — 5

22 Mar MEXICAN, Mexico City
A. Senna — R
G. Berger — 4

5 Apr BRAZILIAN, Interlagos
A. Senna — R
G. Berger — R

3 May SPANISH, Barcelona
A. Senna — 9*
G. Berger — 4

17 May SAN MARINO, Imola
A. Senna — 3
G. Berger — R

31 May MONACO, Monte Carlo
A. Senna — 1
G. Berger — R

14 Jun CANADIAN, Montreal
A. Senna — R
G. Berger — 1

5 Jul FRENCH, Magny-Cours
A. Senna — R
G. Berger — R

12 Jul BRITISH, Silverstone
A. Senna — R
G. Berger — 5

26 Jul GERMAN, Hockenheim
A. Senna — 2
G. Berger — R

16 Aug HUNGARIAN, Hungaroring
A. Senna — 1
G. Berger — 3

30 Aug BELGIAN, Spa
A. Senna — 5
G. Berger — R

13 Sep ITALIAN, Monza
A. Senna — 1
G. Berger — 4

27 Sep PORTUGUESE, Estoril
A. Senna — 3
G. Berger — 2

25 Oct JAPANESE, Suzuka
A. Senna — R
G. Berger — 2

8 Nov AUSTRALIAN, Adelaide
A. Senna — R
G. Berger — 1

1993

McLaren-Ford MP4/8

14 Mar SOUTH AFRICAN, Kyalami
M. Andretti — R
A. Senna — 2

28 Mar BRAZILIAN, Interlagos
M. Andretti — R
A. Senna — 1

11 Apr EUROPEAN, Donington
M. Andretti — R
A. Senna — 1

25 Apr SAN MARINO, Imola
M. Andretti — R
A. Senna — R

9 May SPANISH, Barcelona
M. Andretti — 5
A. Senna — 2

23 May MONACO, Monte Carlo
M. Andretti — 8
A. Senna — 1

13 Jun CANADIAN, Montreal
M. Andretti — 14
A. Senna — 18*

4 Jul FRENCH, Magny-Cours
M. Andretti — 6
A. Senna — 4

11 Jul BRITISH, Silverstone
M. Andretti — R
A. Senna — 5*

25 Jul GERMAN, Hockenheim
M. Andretti — R
A. Senna — 4

15 Aug HUNGARIAN, Hungaroring
M. Andretti — R
A. Senna — R
29 Aug BELGIAN, Spa
M. Andretti — 8
A. Senna — 4
12 Sep ITALIAN, Monza
M. Andretti — 3
A. Senna — R
26 Sep PORTUGUESE, Estoril
M. Hakkinen — R
A. Senna — R
24 Oct JAPANESE, Suzuka
M. Hakkinen — 3
A. Senna — 1
7 Nov AUSTRALIAN, Adelaide
M. Hakkinen — R
A. Senna — 1

1994

McLaren-Peugeot MP4/9

27 Mar BRAZILIAN, Interlagos
M. Hakkinen — R
M. Brundle — R
17 Apr PACIFIC, Aida
M. Hakkinen — R
M. Brundle — R
1 May SAN MARINO, Imola
M. Hakkinen — 3
M. Brundle — 8
15 May MONACO, Monte Carlo
M. Hakkinen — R
M. Brundle — 2
29 May SPANISH, Barcelona
M. Hakkinen — R
M. Brundle — 11*
12 Jun CANADIAN, Montreal
M. Hakkinen — R
M. Brundle — R
3 Jul FRENCH, Magny-Cours
M. Hakkinen — R
M. Brundle — R
10 Jul BRITISH, Silverstone
M. Hakkinen — 3
M. Brundle — R
31 Jul GERMAN, Hockenheim
M. Hakkinen — R
M. Brundle — R
14 Aug HUNGARIAN, Hungaroring
P. Alliot — R
M. Brundle — 4
28 Aug BELGIAN, Spa
M. Hakkinen — 2
M. Brundle — R
11 Sep ITALIAN, Monza
M. Hakkinen — 3
M. Brundle — 5
25 Sep PORTUGUESE, Estoril
M. Hakkinen — 3
M. Brundle — 6
16 Oct EUROPEAN, Jerez
M. Hakkinen — 3
M. Brundle — R

6 Nov JAPANESE, Suzuka
M. Hakkinen — 7
M. Brundle — R
13 Nov AUSTRALIAN, Adelaide
M. Hakkinen — 12*
M. Brundle — 3

1995

McLaren-Mercedes MP4/10 (Brazil-Argentina; Hakkinen, San Marino-Spain); McLaren-Mercedes MP4/10B (Monaco-Australia; Mansell, San Marino-Spain)

26 Mar BRAZILIAN, Interlagos
M. Blundell — 6
M. Hakkinen — 4
9 Apr ARGENTINE, Buenos Aires
M. Blundell — R
M. Hakkinen — R
30 Apr SAN MARINO, Imola
N. Mansell — 10
M. Hakkinen — 5
14 May SPANISH, Barcelona
N. Mansell — R
M. Hakkinen — R
28 May MONACO, Monte Carlo
M. Blundell, 10B — 5
M. Hakkinen, 10B — R
11 Jun CANADIAN, Montreal
M. Blundell — R
M. Hakkinen — R
2 Jul FRENCH, Magny-Cours
M. Blundell — 11
M. Hakkinen — 7
16 Jul BRITISH, Silverstone
M. Blundell — 5
M. Hakkinen — R
30 Jul GERMAN, Hockenheim
M. Blundell — R
M. Hakkinen — R
13 Aug HUNGARIAN, Hungaroring
M. Blundell — R
M. Hakkinen — R
27 Aug BELGIAN, Spa
M. Blundell — 5
M. Hakkinen — R
10 Sep ITALIAN, Monza
M. Blundell — 4
M. Hakkinen — 2
24 Sep PORTUGUESE, Estoril
M. Blundell — 9
M. Hakkinen — R
1 Oct EUROPEAN, Nurburgring
M. Blundell — R
M. Hakkinen — 8
22 Oct PACIFIC, Aida
M. Blundell — 9
J. Magnussen — 10
29 Oct JAPANESE, Suzuka
M. Blundell — 7
M. Hakkinen — 2
12 Nov AUSTRALIAN, Adelaide
M. Blundell — 4
M. Hakkinen — S

1996

McLaren-Mercedes MP4/11

10 Mar AUSTRALIAN, Melbourne
M. Hakkinen — 5
D. Coulthard — R
31 Mar BRAZILIAN, Interlagos
M. Hakkinen — 4
D. Coulthard — R
7 Apr ARGENTINE, Buenos Aires
M. Hakkinen — R
D. Coulthard — 7
28 Apr EUROPEAN, Nurburgring
M. Hakkinen — 8
D. Coulthard — 3
5 May SAN MARINO, Imola
M. Hakkinen — 8*
D. Coulthard — R
19 May MONACO, Monte Carlo
M. Hakkinen — 6*
D. Coulthard — 2
2 Jun SPANISH, Barcelona
M. Hakkinen — 5
D. Coulthard — R
16 Jun CANADIAN, Montreal
M. Hakkinen — 5
D. Coulthard — 4
30 Jun FRENCH, Magny-Cours
M. Hakkinen — 5
D. Coulthard — 6
14 Jul BRITISH, Silverstone
M. Hakkinen — 3
D. Coulthard — 5
28 Jul GERMAN, Hockenheim
M. Hakkinen — R
D. Coulthard — 5
11 Aug HUNGARIAN, Hungaroring
M. Hakkinen — 4
D. Coulthard — R
25 Aug BELGIAN, Spa
M. Hakkinen — 3
D. Coulthard — R
8 Sep ITALIAN, Monza
M. Hakkinen — 3
D. Coulthard — R
22 Sep PORTUGUESE, Estoril
M. Hakkinen — R
D. Coulthard — 13
13 Oct JAPANESE, Suzuka
M. Hakkinen — 3
D. Coulthard — 8

1997

McLaren-Mercedes MP4/12

9 Mar AUSTRALIAN, Melbourne
M. Hakkinen — 3
D. Coulthard — 1
30 Mar BRAZILIAN, Interlagos
M. Hakkinen — 4
D. Coulthard — 10
13 Apr ARGENTINE, Buenos Aires
M. Hakkinen — 5
D. Coulthard — R

27 Apr SAN MARINO, Imola
  M. Hakkinen   6
  D. Coulthard   R
11 May MONACO, Monte Carlo
  M. Hakkinen   R
  D. Coulthard   R
25 May SPANISH, Barcelona
  M. Hakkinen   7
  D. Coulthard   6
15 Jun CANADIAN, Montreal
  M. Hakkinen   R
  D. Coulthard   7
29 Jun FRENCH, Magny-Cours
  M. Hakkinen   R
  D. Coulthard   7*
13 Jul BRITISH, Silverstone
  M. Hakkinen   R
  D. Coulthard   4
27 Jul GERMAN, Hockenheim
  M. Hakkinen   3
  D. Coulthard   R
10 Aug HUNGARIAN, Hungaroring
  M. Hakkinen   R
  D. Coulthard   R
24 Aug BELGIAN, Spa
  M. Hakkinen   D
  D. Coulthard   R
7 Sep ITALIAN, Monza
  M. Hakkinen   9
  D. Coulthard   1
21 Sep AUSTRIAN, A1-Ring
  M. Hakkinen   R
  D. Coulthard   2
28 Sep LUXEMBOURG, Nurburgring
  M. Hakkinen   R
  D. Coulthard   R
12 Oct JAPANESE, Suzuka
  M. Hakkinen   4
  D. Coulthard   10*
26 Oct EUROPEAN, Jerez
  M. Hakkinen   1
  D. Coulthard   2

1998
McLaren-Mercedes MP4/13

8 Mar AUSTRALIAN, Melbourne
  D. Coulthard   2
  M. Hakkinen   1
29 Mar BRAZILIAN, Interlagos
  D. Coulthard   2
  M. Hakkinen   1

12 Apr ARGENTINE, Buenos Aires
  D. Coulthard   6
  M. Hakkinen   2
26 Apr SAN MARINO, Imola
  D. Coulthard   1
  M. Hakkinen   R
10 May SPANISH, Barcelona
  D. Coulthard   2
  M. Hakkinen   1
24 May MONACO, Monte Carlo
  D. Coulthard   R
  M. Hakkinen   1
7 Jun CANADIAN, Montreal
  D. Coulthard   R
  M. Hakkinen   R
28 Jun FRENCH, Magny-Cours
  D. Coulthard   6
  M. Hakkinen   3
12 Jul BRITISH, Silverstone
  D. Coulthard   R
  M. Hakkinen   2
26 Jul AUSTRIAN, A1-Ring
  D. Coulthard   2
  M. Hakkinen   1
2 Aug GERMAN, Hockenheim
  D. Coulthard   2
  M. Hakkinen   1
16 Aug HUNGARIAN, Hungaroring
  D. Coulthard   2
  M. Hakkinen   6
30 Aug BELGIAN, Spa
  D. Coulthard   7
  M. Hakkinen   R
13 Sep ITALIAN, Monza
  D. Coulthard   R
  M. Hakkinen   4
27 Sep LUXEMBOURG, Nurburgring
  D. Coulthard   3
  M. Hakkinen   1
1 Nov JAPANESE, Suzuka
  D. Coulthard   3
  M. Hakkinen   1

1999
McLaren-Mercedes MP4/14

7 Mar AUSTRALIAN, Melbourne
  M. Hakkinen   R
  D. Coulthard   R

11 Apr BRAZILIAN, Interlagos
  M. Hakkinen   1
  D. Coulthard   R
2 May SAN MARINO, Imola
  M. Hakkinen   R
  D. Coulthard   2
16 May MONACO, Monte Carlo
  M. Hakkinen   3
  D. Coulthard   R
30 May SPANISH, Barcelona
  M. Hakkinen   1
  D. Coulthard   2
13 Jun CANADIAN, Montreal
  M. Hakkinen   1
  D. Coulthard   7
27 Jun FRENCH, Magny-Cours
  M. Hakkinen   2
  D. Coulthard   R
11 Jul BRITISH, Silverstone
  M. Hakkinen   R
  D. Coulthard   1
25 Jul AUSTRIA, A1-Ring
  M. Hakkinen   3
  D. Coulthard   2
1 Aug GERMANY, Hockenheim
  M. Hakkinen   R
  D. Coulthard   5
15 Aug HUNGARY, Hungaroring
  M. Hakkinen   1
  D. Coulthard   2
29 Aug BELGIUM, Spa
  M. Hakkinen   2
  D. Coulthard   1
12 Sep ITALY, Monza
  M. Hakkinen   R
  D. Coulthard   5
26 Sep EUROPEAN, Nurburgring
  M. Hakkinen   5
  D. Coulthard   R
17 Oct MALAYSIA, Sepang
  M. Hakkinen   3
  D. Coulthard   R
31 Oct JAPAN, Suzuka
  M. Hakkinen   1
  D. Coulthard   R

Appendix 2

McLaren – team statistics

RECORD TO END OF 1999
(*from 1973 when first built cars under own name*)

Grands Prix contested: 492
Pole positions: 103
Victories: 123
Fastest race laps: 88

CONSTRUCTORS' CHAMPIONSHIP PLACINGS:

1973	–	10th	2 points
1966	–	7th	3 points
1967	–	8th	1 point
1968	–	2nd	51 points
1969	–	4th	40 points
1970	–	4th	35 points
1971	–	6th	10 points
1972	–	3rd	47 points
1973	–	3rd	58 points
1974	–	1st	73 points
1975	–	3rd	53 points
1976	–	2nd	74 points
1977	–	3rd	60 points
1978	–	8th	15 points
1979	–	7th	15 points
1980	–	7th	11 points
1981	–	6th	28 points
1982	–	2nd	69 points
1983	–	5th	34 points
1984	–	1st	143.5 points
1985	–	1st	90 points
1986	–	2nd	96 points
1987	–	2nd	76 points
1988	–	1st	199 points
1989	–	1st	141 points
1990	–	1st	121 points
1991	–	1st	139 points
1992	–	2nd	99 points
1993	–	2nd	84 points
1994	–	4th	42 points
1995	–	4th	30 points
1996	–	4th	49 points
1997	–	4th	63 points
1998	–	1st	156 points
1999	–	2nd	124 points

Appendix

McLaren –
most successful drivers

DAVID COULTHARD (GB) Born
27.3.71. F1 debut, 1994, Spain (Williams).
Drove for McLaren 1996 to date. Seven
career wins, six with McLaren.

EMERSON FITTIPALDI (BR). Born
12.12.46. F1 debut, 1970, Britain (Lotus).
Drove for McLaren 1974–75. 14 career
wins, five with McLaren. World Champion
1972 (Lotus) and 74 (McLaren).

MIKA HAKKINEN (FIN) Born 28.9.68.
F1 debut, 1991, US West (Lotus). Drove
for McLaren 1993 to date. 14 career wins,
all with McLaren. World Champion 1998
and 1999.

DENNY HULME (NZ). Born 18.6.36,
died 4.10.92. F1 debut 1965, Monaco
(Brabham). Drove for McLaren 1968–74.
Eight career wins, six with McLaren.
World Champion 1967 (Brabham).

JAMES HUNT (GB). Born 29.8.47, died
15.6.93. F1 debut 1973 Monaco (March).
Drove for McLaren 1976–78. Ten career
wins, nine with McLaren. World
Champion 1976.

JOCHEN MASS (D). Born 30.9.46. F1
debut, 1973 Britain (Surtees). Drove for
McLaren 1976 to 77. One career win with
McLaren.

BRUCE McLAREN (NZ). Born 30.8.37,
died 2.6.70. F1 debut, 1958 German
(Cooper). Drove for McLaren 1966 to 70.
Four career wins, one with McLaren.

ALAIN PROST (F). Born 24.2.55. F1
debut 1980 Brazil (McLaren). Drove for
McLaren 1980 and 1984–89. 51 career
wins, 30 with McLaren. World Champion
1985, 86, 89 (McLaren) and 93
(Williams).

AYRTON SENNA (BR). Born 21.3.60,
died 1.5.94. F1 debut 1984 Brazil
(Toleman). Drove for McLaren 1988–93.
41 career wins, 35 with McLaren. World
Champion 1988, 90 and 91 (McLaren).

JOHN WATSON (GB). Born 4.5.46. F1
debut, 1973, Britain (Brabham). Drove
for McLaren 1979 to 83. Five career wins,
four with McLaren.

OTHER BOOKS OF INTEREST

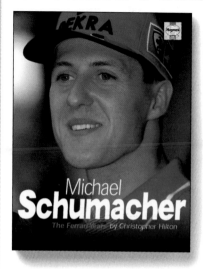

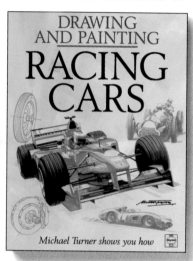

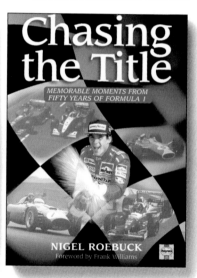

AUDIO CASSETTES A collection of audio cassettes featuring top Formula 1 drivers is available from **Audiosport Ltd**, The Fairway, Bush Fair, Harlow, Essex CM18 6LY (tel: 01279 444707). Scripted by Christopher Hilton and narrated by Julian Harries, the Grand Prix Heroes series includes cassettes on Jacques Villeneuve, Michael Schumacher, Mika Hakkinen and Johnny Herbert.

For more information on books please contact: Customer Services, Haynes Publishing, Sparkford, Nr Yeovil, Somerset BA22 7JJ
Tel. 01963 440635 **Fax:** 01963 440001
Int. tel: +44 1963 440635 **Fax:** +44 1963 440001
E-mail: sales@haynes-manuals.co.uk **Web site:** www.haynes.co.uk